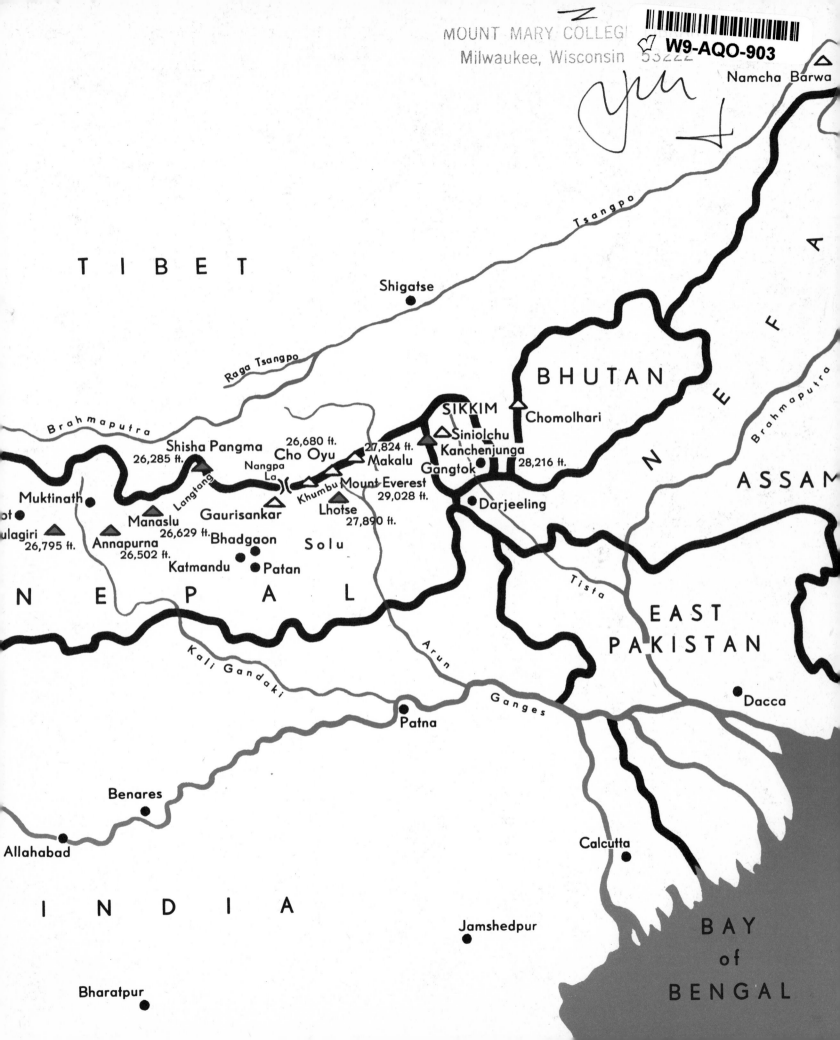

Namcha Barwa

TIBET

Tsangpo

Shigatse

Raga Tsangpo

BHUTAN

N E F A

Brahmaputra

SIKKIM

Chomolhari

Shisha Pangma
26,285 ft.

26,680 ft.
Cho Oyu

27,824 ft.
Makalu

Siniolchu
Kanchenjunga
28,216 ft.

Nangpa
La

Gangtok

ASSAM

Langtang

Khumbu
Mount Everest
29,028 ft.

Brahmaputra

Muktinath

Darjeeling

Gaurisankar

Lhotse
27,890 ft.

ot

Manaslu

Dhaulagiri
26,795 ft.

Annapurna
26,502 ft.

26,629 ft.
Bhadgaon

Solu

Tista

EAST
PAKISTAN

Katmandu

Patan

N E P A L

Dacca

Kali Gandaki

Arun

Ganges

Patna

Benares

Calcutta

Allahabad

I N D I A

Jamshedpur

BAY
of
BENGAL

Bharatpur

Herbert Tichy

HIMALAYA

Herbert Tichy

HIMALAYA

G. P. Putnam's Sons

New York

The frontispiece by the Sherpa artist Kalden shows his home village in the Himalayas. It stands at the foot of Mount Khumbila, which is so sacred to the Sherpas that no member of their tribe has ever set foot on its summit. Above the village, lamas and lay brothers are seen at prayer before a shrine bedecked with flags. Inside the village, surrounded by houses, stands a Buddhist temple. Women with huge burdens on their backs move through the streets, while cattle graze near chortens, Lamaist monuments in which sacred relics are preserved.

The photographs in this book were supplied by the following photographers and services:

Alpinismus, Munich: Illus. 123, 125, 128; Karl Ambichl, Hieflau: Illus. 44, 46; Wolfgang Axt, St. Johann: Illus. 7, 67; Bavaria-Verlag, Munich: Illus. 83; Jan Boon, Kitzbühel: Illus. 3, 33, 34, 70, 76, 81, 85; Peter Breuer, Durlach: Illus. 38, 39, 66; Deutsche Himalayagesellschaft, Munich: Illus. 43, 106, 108, 114, 116, 117, 118, 119, 120; Kurt Diemberger, Salzburg: Illus. 13, 100, 102, 110, 112, 126; Norman Dyhrenfurth, Riggenberg: Illus. 1, 53, 80; Mario Fantin, Bologna: Illus. 112, 113, 121; Günter Hauser, Munich: Illus. 12, 55, 73, 78, 95; Helmut Heuberger, Innsbruck: Illus. 10, 11, 28, 30, 31, 35, 52, 71, 77; Istitutio di Fotografia Alpina V. Sella: Illus. 104, 105; Sepp Jöchler, Hall in Tirol: Illus. 32; Gerhart Klamert, Munich: Illus. 5, 42, 79; Lino Lacedelli, Cortina d'Ampezzo: Illus. 127; Fritz Lohbichler, Oberstdorf: Illus. 8, 26, 50, 51, 91, 92, 96, 97, 99; The Mount Everest Foundation, London: Illus. 103; Österreichische Himalayagesellschaft, Vienna: Illus. 37, 49, 88; Erich Reismüller, Berg bei Starnberg: Illus. 75, 115; Markus Schmuck, Salzburg: Illus. 109; Erwin Schneider, Hall in Tirol: Illus. 4; Herbert Tichy, Vienna: Illus. 2, 6, 9, 14, 15, 16, 17, 18, 19, 20, 21, 22, 23, 24, 25, 26, 27, 29, 36, 41, 45, 47, 48, 54, 56, 57, 59, 60, 61, 62, 63, 64, 65, 68, 69, 72, 74, 82, 84, 86, 87, 89, 90, 94, 124, 129; Erich Vanis, Vienna: Illus. 58, 98, 101; Fritz Wintersteller, Salzburg: Illus. 111; Zentrale Farbbild-Agentur, Düsseldorf: Illus. 40, 93

The endpaper map is by Ella Goldschmidt, Vienna

The plates were prepared by Klischeeanstalt Beissner & Co., Vienna

Printed by Christoph Reisser's Söhne AG, Vienna

This edition copyright © 1970 by Anton Schroll & Co., Vienna

Translated by Richard Rickett and David Streatfeild

German language edition copyright © 1968 by Anton Schroll & Co., Vienna

Library of Congress Catalog Card Number: 74-92806
Printed in Austria

Contents

The Himalayas Have Many Faces

The Himalayas have many characteristics that are not shared by other mountains. I saw the one that made the deepest impression on me in June, 1950, from Darjeeling. At this time of year one naturally expected the monsoons, the season of billowing mists and violent rain, but what happened in 1950 was a catastrophe: For two days, without stopping, the water lashed down on the earth. Thirty-nine inches fell in Darjeeling, 10 more in the surrounding villages.

The earth could not stand up to this hammering. Not only did the mountain torrents tear away boulders and uproot trees, but the rock itself lost that permanence which we take for granted: mountainsides began to fall away, and landslides tore up the earth. From a lama temple came the incessant booming of a gong, for the mountain below seemed to be sinking into the earth; destruction seemed imminent when at last the movement was halted, only a few yards from the temple wall: Prayer had prevailed. Those who had prayed were full of faith and experienced in the service of the Himalayan gods, for did they not see the great god of the Kanchenjunga before them every clear morning? Ordinary mortals were less fortunate; 120 perished, and hundreds of houses were destroyed. All was mourning and despair.

I had no time to wait to share the revival of new hope in the town. I was bound for the western Himalayas and had come to Darjeeling only to find a suitable Sherpa as my companion for the next few months. I found Nima Tensing, a young daredevil all agog for new mountains, and I too was longing to set out. There was nothing to keep us.

But both the railway and the road which connected Darjeeling with the plains were cut and unusable, and it might take months to repair them. We had to go down on foot, and it was a hard and melancholy march, past ruins that had once been houses, mud streams that had been fields of rice and corn. An old peasant, taking me no doubt for an Englishman and evidently no supporter of Nehru's government, said reproachfully "It never rained like this under your raj!"

Toward evening—we had not progressed very far—the weather cleared and the sun broke through. Below us lay the Indian plain. In the winter season it is a lifeless gray flat over which the wind spreads a veil of dust as though the earth were ashamed to show its open wounds, but after the rains a green fertile carpet stretching to the horizon—always a fascinating sight, revealing as it does the greatness of India, its riches and its poverty.

Now a sea stretched out below us. The water was not deep, for trees and the roofs of houses rose above the surface, but as far as the eye could see, the earth had disappeared.

We squatted down for a rest on the damp ground, and Nima said, "Much, much water!" And I dreamed that the earth had grown several million years younger and that I was privileged to watch it as it made ready to throw up the highest mountain system in the world. The rigid block of the Angara landmass was drifting infinitely slowly but with incalculable force against the Gondwana landmass, and between them lay the Himalaya Sea, the Tethys. The peninsula we now call India was either seabed or part of the Gondwana landmass. This continental drift, discovered and so named by Alfred Wegener, raised the seabed so that the Tethys flattened out, and on its northern shore the stratum folds were driven upward. The Himalayan mountain group, the most recent in the world, thus began its growth. Rivers carried its rubble down, covering the former seabed with it. The subcontinent of India was joined to the Asian landmass, and the Himalaya Sea vanished, surviving only in the minds of investigators and in the fossils of its strata.

But in this moment the remote past had become present; 50,000,000 to 70,000,000 years had still to run their course. The Himalaya Sea glittered wide and eternal in the rays of the sinking sun, just as though it were not destined to change back so soon into a landscape of plowed fields. The development of man and his capacity for making tools, the era of the great migrations, and the brief moment we call history, with its hungry peasants, mighty conquerors and great saints—all that was washed away in the ocean of the past and now awaited its time to materialize. What other mountains can reveal the marvel of their birth? I have never known the Himalayas so impressive.

Four years later it was granted me to undergo an experience that brought the height of the Himalayas home. We were climbing down from the peak of the Cho Oyu (26,680 feet) by way of its northeastern face to our Camp 4. The day had been tiring and bitterly cold; setting out at sunrise, we had climbed 4,000 feet. For a long time we had not known whether we would reach the summit, and when we did, we were in doubt whether it would be possible to regain the shelter of the tent before nightfall, but now we were sure the day was going to end well.

The joy of having reached the summit drove out fatigue. When Pasang, who had been in charge of bringing up our supplies and had a unique performance to his credit, reached the top, the tears had run down his cheeks, and he had only been able to whisper again and again the word "peak." His emotion was understandable, for as a sirdar he had long striven for a "high peak," by which he meant the first ascent of a 25,000-footer. The tears were unfortunate, for in the icy wind they froze, increasing the danger of frostbite.

Sepp Jöchler and I were hardly more talkative than he. That was due not only to fatigue but also to the dry air with its low oxygen content at over 25,000 feet, which confined us to hoarse whispers. In any case, what words would have been adequate?

It was a cloudless late-autumn day with visibility to a great distance northward. Below us, behind a reddish haze which the approaching night spread over the depths, lay the highlands of Tibet— "the roof of the world." We knew we had been on a "high peak," for at that time the Cho Oyu was the third highest peak yet scaled, and it is the seventh highest in the world. Those were mere

1 File of porters at
the foot of Mount Nuptse

figures or facts that one appreciated in the form of the labor of each step and the gasping for breath; now the height really meant something, for we were descending to the roof of the world. There it lay below us, much farther below than the floods I had seen in Bengal had lain, and the hilly landscape, flattened by the low shadows, was also reminiscent of a sea, but one whose purple surface lay 13,000 feet higher than the muddy water had. Now the height came as a direct experience to me, not as feet above sea level or geographical names, but in the fact that we were having to stagger painfully downward to the highest level to which other people aspired in their dreams. On that occasion I saw an aspect of the Himalayas which no other mountains possess in the same degree, for from the others one climbs down into valleys, not onto the roof of the world.

There was a third experience; one might find it in other mountains, but never with the same magnificence and beauty. It came at the end of a four months' expedition across Nepal; I was accompanied by four Sherpas, and during this time I had heard no news of happenings in the world and had seen no other white man. For all its geographical variety my world had grown very small. Would we find enough provisions in the next village? Would the bridge that we had been counting on for days still be usable, or had it been swept away in the last spate? Would the approach of winter deny us the hoped-for peaks, edging us away toward the warmer south? We had luck: Provisions, bridges, and peaks were all available.

The view to the south was overwhelming, out beyond the mountain waves to the wide skyline formed by the haze and dust over the Indian plain. The number of mountain chains varied with the clarity of the air and the sun's elevation; once I counted twenty-six, although I could not distinguish the lower ones. In every valley, or nearly everyone, there lived human beings such as I had already met, and under the haze lay workaday India, with its poverty and fatalism, its usurers and saints, maharajas and beggars. Perhaps the only reason this view fascinated me, seducing me to take a rest which Pasang did not consider necessary, was that I loved India, and the haze veiled or suggested a continent with a population of 400,000,000. Where else can one see a continent from a peak?

It was the end of our pilgrimage; the next day we would reach India. Many people passed—no longer the proud figures of the lonely high valleys, but types that one sees in bazaars and railway stations. But the view did not agree with that, and as though to make the parting harder, it summarized all the beauties of the past months in one tremendous picture: to the north the high peaks, from the Kamet to Dhaulagiri, were visible to a distance of 200 miles—men of experience have assured me that there is no finer view in the Lower Himalayas than that from Pithoragarh—while to the south lay the endless mountain chains and valleys.

Influenced perhaps by a perverse pleasure in prolonging the inevitable parting, I had dropped behind the Sherpas when I was startled by the wailing voice of a blind beggar squatting by the wayside. I had no money with me, but in my rucksack there were some cigarettes, a handful of tobacco, and a warm shirt. While I hunted for these things and placed them in the beggar's hands, without raising my eyes from his avid fingers I felt the beauty of the Himalayas with agonizing sharpness. I and the pictures in this book will attempt to describe and illustrate it, but we both shall fail.

Perhaps I shall come nearest to conveying what I mean when I say that I have seen many blind people: by the sea, in towns, among smiling hills, in a Persian village that seemed to be exclusively

10

inhabited by blind people who came running after the sound of every gasoline engine like emaciated, begging ghosts. It was always horrible and left me wondering by what justice sight was taken from one and left to another.

But the beggar in Pithoragarh shook me so painfully that a chill ran through me.

That is how beautiful the Himalayas are.

All the Zones of the Earth

The Himalayas are 1,500 miles in length, or about twice as long as the Alps, and Mount Everest is nearly twice as high as the Matterhorn. The name comes from Sanscrit *hima*, snow, and *ālaya*, home; the accent is on the second syllable. Strictly speaking, the Himalayas extend from the valley of the Indus to that of the Brahmaputra, from the western bastion Nanga Parbat (26,629 feet) to the eastern outpost Namcha Barwa (25,400 feet). As a mountaineer rather than a geographer, one is inclined to include the river valleys of Indochina to the south, as well as the Pamirs, the Karakorum, and the Hindu Kush in this mountain system. To the superficial observer, particularly if he flies over them in a few hours, all these form a unity.

An Indian poet gave an even wider definition, saying that the Persians see the most westerly, the Chinese the most easterly outposts of the great Central Asian mountain system—and had not all these peaks the right to be called "Home of the snows?"

Following this definition, in dealing with "the Himalayas" we shall not confine ourselves to their geographical limits but will attempt to show their beauty, describe their peculiarities, and relate what they have meant to humanity, from the writers of the ancient Indian Vedas to the peak hunters of the most recent decades. The mountaineers will not get so much space, for nearly 2,000 years ago the Indian poet Kalidasa produced finer praise of the Himalayas than the reports of modern expeditions succeed in doing. We cannot give a comprehensive account of all the inhabitants of the mountains but shall confine ourselves to a few groups who are conspicuous by reason of peculiarities in their way of life. This book is not intended as a monograph on the Himalayas, but rather as a record of personal experiences, of the fates of others, and of the landscape in which it all happened.

Of the 14 mountains over 26,200 feet, 10 are in the Himalayas, the remaining 4—K 2, Hidden Peak, Broad Peak, and Gasherbrum II—in the neighboring Karakorum. The majority of the 300 over 23,000 feet are also in the Himalayas, and all of them in Asia. No other mountain system has such high or such difficult passes as the Himalayas, which, all in all, may claim with justice to be "the premier mountains of the world."

The central sector, reaching from Kashmir to Bhutan, forms a real climatic barrier, dividing the dry uplands of Tibet from the rainy, sometimes even tropical southern slopes. In the eastern spurs, on the other hand, where the monsoon from the Bay of Bengal dashes itself with its full force against the mountain wall and runs into a kind of dead end in Assam, not only do the lower valleys receive vast quantities of rain, but the moisture is carried by the strength of the wind right over the crest, penetrating deep into the Asian landmass.

In the west the situation is reversed, as typified in the Indus Valley. In the course of its 1,000-mile passage westward the monsoon loses its original titanic force, and the rainfall it brings decreases, while the torrid Indian sun opposes and finally overcomes it. The tropical rain forests of Assam and Sikkim are succeeded first by humid and finally by dry deciduous woods, and these are followed by the thorn-grown steppes of the Punjab, and finally the desert landscape of the Indus Valley, wooded only on its higher slopes. Thus it is only in the central sector that the Himalayas form a dividing line between two climates and vegetation types; in the east the monsoon is too strong to be halted by the barrier, in the west too weak to bring high rainfall to the southern slopes.

When the German Nanga Parbat expedition of 1934 under Willi Merkl was brought to a tragic end by a monsoon disaster—in addition to Merkl, two German members of the expedition and six high-altitude porters perished—there was talk of a "killer monsoon." The latest investigations and discoveries of the climatologists suggest that the disaster was not in fact caused by the already weakened monsoon, but by influxes of cold air from the so-called West-Wind Belt. Fritz Bechtold's report on the 1934 expedition states that "the snowstorm came definitely from the west, as is the case with all sudden changes of the weather from April to August inclusive." The well-known Himalaya expert Paul Bauer also spoke subsequently of "falls of snow approaching from the west." The headlines Monsoon on Nanga Parbat which appeared throughout the world at the time thus in fact constituted a false report.

The next German Nanga Parbat expedition (1937) came to an even more terrible end, for which perhaps lack of local knowledge was partly responsible. In their Camp 4 seven sahibs and nine Sherpas were buried and killed in the night by an avalanche.

A year later, when I was climbing with Pasang Dawa Lama—of whom I shall have much to say—in western Nepal, he asserted that this disaster might have been avoided. We were seeking a suitable camping place for the night on a trough-shaped glacier. Little fresh snow was lying, and the slopes seemed to offer no danger of landslides, so that Pasang's excessive carefulness gave me the impression of being calculated rather to impress me with his prudent planning than to avert any real danger. When I gave voice to this suspicion, Pasang was genuinely angry. "If sleeping here," he said reproachfully, "then you dying here, like other sahibs who always knowing better."

I inquired to which better-knowing shaibs he referred. He explained that on Nanga Parbat, before Camp 4 was set up on the spot chosen for it, the Sherpas had given warning that there was danger of landslides, but the sahibs had known better and had taken no notice. What could the Sherpas do? "They died," he added reproachfully.

12

2

3

"How can you know that?" I asked. "There were no survivors to say what happened."

But Pasang corrected me, claiming that one Sherpa had turned back after the camp was set up, surviving to tell of the sahibs' imprudence.

I had no means of checking the truth of this story of Pasang's, but I made no further resistance to the pedantic exactitude with which he set up the tent. During the bitterly cold night that followed I came to appreciate his carefulness, for the glacier, hitherto silent and peaceable, became threatening and noisy. The tremendous fall in temperature—for the day had been scorching—set up such stresses in the ice that fragments burst from the steep sides with the sound of shots, and small avalanches of ice cataracted down like mountain streams. Pasang was generous enough not to make play with the triumph of his superior experience—he would in any case have had to exert himself very considerably to make himself heard in the din—and I had learned that the Himalayas have their own laws.

Another peculiarity of this mightiest mountain range in the world is that it does not form a watershed, for several rivers, following awe-inspiring gorges, force their way through it from north to south. The Indus and the Brahmaputra, which both rise near the sacred Mount Kailas in Tibet, first follow east-west and west-east courses respectively, as though seeking a weak spot in the mountain barrier through which to pursue their way to the Indian Ocean. Between these two great rivers a number of smaller ones with sources on the north, in Tibet, find their way through the Himalayas. The actual watershed between the Indian Ocean and the undrained Central Asian basin follows approximately the course of the Sven Hedin range and lies some 100 to 125 miles north of the principal chain of the Himalayas.

Two theories have been advanced to account for this river penetration. The antecedence theory maintains that the rivers are older than the mountains and, while the latter were being forced up the rivers, had time to eat their way ever more deeply into the rock. A proof of this theory is claimed in the fact that some of the rivers have not selected a course through soft rock strata but break through crystalline base rock—for instance the Arun, east of Mount Everest, the upper reaches of which cut through strata of gneiss.

The theory of retrogressive erosion explains the narrow breaches by the speed with which the Himalayas grew and by the heavy monsoon rainfall on the southern slopes, as a result of which the rivers dispose of so much water and such steep gradients that they can accomplish more than those in other mountains. They also produce landscapes of incomparable scenic grandeur. Thus for instance the peaks of Dhaulagiri and Annapurna, both over 26,000 feet, are only 22 miles apart, but between them the valley of the Kali Gandaki reaches an altitude of only 4,000 feet—a difference of 22,000 feet between peak and valley. The courses washed out by the rivers during the more recent upheaval of the Himalayas, which was vertical, are like gorges: The valley sides have only a shallow gradient at the top and then plunge vertically down to the riverbed. Since in the Himalayas the tracks follow the valleys, and during the monsoons many rivers carry a volume of water as much as sixty times as great as in the dry period, a great number of bridges have to be rebuilt after every spate, so that communications in the valleys are often interrupted for months.

If the retrogressive erosion maintains its force, the maps will have to be revised quite soon—

"soon" geologically speaking. The northernmost tributary of the Arun rises only a few miles from the Tsangpo; if its source shifts farther northwards, it will tap the latter one day, saving its upper waters the wide detour to the Namcha Barwa by enabling them to flow past Mount Everest into the Ganges. Perhaps other rivers situated farther westward, such as the Kali Gandaki mentioned above, will also work their way northward with the same rapidity, providing the Tsangpo with yet more outlets to India. In that case the mighty Brahmaputra, which is the name of the Tsangpo on its way through India to the Bay of Bengal, will be reduced to a wretched stream, flowing like a gutter rill down the middle of the shimmering sand flats of its former bed.

But in the meanwhile scientists have abandoned as untenable the theory of retrogressive erosion as the primary cause of the river breaches through the Himalayas.

Geographers have adopted a division of the Himalayas from west to east along the major rivers rising in the range as follows:

Punjab Himalayas (Himachal Pradesh)	from Indus to Sutlej	about 370 miles
Kumaun Himalayas	from Sutlej to Kali	about 220 miles
Nepal Himalayas	from Kali to Tista	about 500 miles
Assam Himalayas	from Tista to Brahmaputra	about 470 miles

The north-south division varies with the preciseness of the geologist and the part of the range with which he is concerned. For our present purposes the following scheme will suffice:

Tibetan Himalayas
High Himalayas
Lower Himalayas

From east to west the fauna and flora exhibit only trifling differences, depending on the varying strength of the monsoons, but in crossing the Himalayas from south to north, one passes through every one of the climatic zones. This is seen with particular impressiveness in Nepal. Along the Indian frontier stretches the long strip of the Terai, a tropical primeval forest with tiger, rhinoceros—and malaria. Then come the mountains and valleys of the Middle Himalayas, in which a temperate climate offers the possibility of every kind of agriculture. Here the majority of the settlements are situated, as well as Katmandu, the capital. As a consequence of overpopulation, the arable land is intensively exploited, and the terraced fields that cover the hilly landscape stretch far up into the mountains. Bananas, oranges, sugarcane, and rice—but also potatoes and wheat—all flourish. It is hoped to raise the agricultural yield materially by the introduction of modern methods, but the mountainous country is unsuited to tractors and other machines, so the peasants will probably have to continue to cultivate their terraced plots, often no more than a yard wide, with the aid of hoes. Whenever one passes through the Middle Himalayas, one notices the thriftiness, even niggardliness of the inhabitants with their precious land. As soon as one comes to rice fields, the path, which had been broad and well trodden in the woodlands, disappears altogether, and travelers must make their arduous way in single file, balancing precariously on the slippery dikes that regulate the water level on the fields. Land is too precious to be squandered on paths.

After this the rhododendron belt begins. More than 200 species have been identified, and they grow up to 50 feet high, transforming the countryside during the flowering season into an enchanted garden. There are red, white, pink, and yellow blossoms, and between them lichens sway, providing a soft background to the orgy of color. Lower down we rested in the shade of banyan trees, and the jungle was so thick that only an occasional ray of sunlight penetrated its roof and reached the ground. It was under a banyan that the Buddha attained enlightenment, and some of them are revered as holy. The roots, which hang from the branches, are reminiscent of the columns of a cathedral.

The woods now grow less luxuriant. Around the villages the trees are felled recklessly, but near the monasteries they are protected, for the lamas believe that trees once sacrificed their lives to save another. They are Boddhisattvas and will one day be reincarnated in human form. No tree seems worthier of such honor than the Himalayan cedar; he who has ever rested in its shade averts his eyes in embarrassment when confronted with the famous cedars of Lebanon.

The meadows resemble those in the Alps, except that here the flowers do not stand out singly against the carpet of grass—their brilliant colors overlay the green. But it is as if one were transported to the Alps, so many old friends does one find; primrose, gentian, campanula, cinquefoil, forget-me-not, poppy, saxifrage, buttercup—all are there. In some places it is impossible to take a step without treading on a couple of edelweiss.

We have now reached the high-altitude passes leading to Tibet. Only a few plants manage to survive between scree and old glacier debris, and the top of the pass itself is covered with snow and ice even at the height of summer. We have come to the end of a journey from tropical forest to a kind of eternal Arctic cap; as the crow flies the distance from start to finish is hardly 125 miles, and we have not crossed the frontier of Nepal. Setting out to explore the Himalayas, we have found samples of the whole world.

Two more peculiarities of the Himalayas may be mentioned. The snow line is often lower on the southern than on the northern slopes. Thus the highest village south of Dhaulagiri lies at only 7,200 feet, while in Phopagaon, on the north, barley and potatoes are grown at 14,100 feet. The main crest with the high peaks precipitates the bulk of the snow and rain of the monsoon on the southern slopes.

From the economic point of view the Himalayas are disappointing; only a few mineral deposits that repay working have been found in them. Some of these would be suitable for small enterprises if it were not for transportation problems. The Himalayas simply do not favor industry.

In Kashmir small quantities of bauxite, coal, and zinc occur, in Sikkim a little copper, in Nepal cobalt and nickel, and in Lahul antimony. There are traces of uranium in the crystalline formations of Kulu and Garhwal. On the south side of the Himalayas, in the western Punjab and in Assam, oil has been found, but its production would have no economic significance.

If one travels in the Himalayas in the capacity of geologist, the local potentates mostly give the necessary permits in the hope that one will discover gold or at least copper, and to keep them well disposed, it is advisable not to damp their optimism too much. One's return is apt to be embarrassing.

5 Suspension bridge over the Hunza River
6 Sunset in the Himalayan foothills in India
7 Camp by night
8 Unmapped peak (20,000 feet), in northwestern Karakorum
9 Nepalese peasants by a stubble field

10 Lama temple in eastern Nepal
11 Rhododendron blossoms in the Mount Everest area
12 Bamboo on the southern slopes of the Himalayas
13 Mount Dhaulagiri (26,795 feet)
14 Millet field in western Nepal

The Home of the Gods

In classical times Europeans knew little about the Himalayas. Herodotus indeed tells of "ants" that dug for gold—perhaps in Tibet?—but for long our knowledge of the Orient was overshadowed by the warnings of Moses and Ezekiel concerning Gog, who ruled over Magog far beyond the Caucasus. They were the enemies who would one day ally themselves with the Persians, the Armenians and other auxiliaries to attack Palestine. The kingdom of God felt itself threatened by unknown peoples from places uncannily remote and feared a visitation on a Biblical scale.

The campaign of Alexander the Great of 327–325 B.C. pierced the mystery that surrounded the mountain land, but before that the Greeks had already suspected that the sources of the Indus and the Ganges lay among very high mountains.

After Alexander, geographical knowledge was rapidly widened and acquired an astonishing accuracy. Megasthenes (c. 300 B.C.) who lived as ambassador at the court of Chandragupta Maurya, introduced the Greeks to the Indian expressions "Emodon" and "Imaon," which they interpreted as the western and eastern Himalayas. Ptolemy (c. A.D. 170) was well informed about the conformation of Asia, although details were still lacking and the Himalayas still a blank space on the map.

After this Europe was for a time fully occupied with internal affairs, and it was not until the Crusades and the journeys of Marco Polo that fresh information became available.

China possessed thoroughly accurate knowledge of the Himalayas long before the West did, and it is surprising to find that this knowledge was not promoted by practical political or economic considerations but by religion. The Chinese travelers who have left accounts of the high passes and the eternal snows were neither warriors nor merchants, but pilgrims.

In China the Han Dynasty (206 B.C.–A.D. 220) had built up a mighty empire based on the teachings of Confucius, by which the position of the individual—his rights over subordinates and his duties to superiors—was precisely fixed. This system was not adequate to maintain the greatness of the empire, however. Many of the emperors were "cosmic pivots of world happening," lacking the personality required to give force to the system, with the result that it was replaced by Taoism.

Taoism is as old as Confucianism and is its polar opposite. Instead of setting each individual in a particular position in an immutable world order, it imposes on him all the liberties and the difficulties of individuality. The Buddhism that had originated in India seemed akin to Taoism, and in

6

7

11

12

13

14

no way opposed to it. It was possible, it was indeed unavoidable, to draw on it in order to revitalize the old system.

In the relationship between these two systems many points remained obscure. Thus the Taoist injunction to practice wu wei, or inaction, was equated with the Buddhist nirvana. The Buddhist canon is so voluminous that our Bible is like a pocket calendar beside it. In order to reinforce Taoism, which had no answer for various religious-philosophical questions, with the riches of Buddhism, Chinese pilgrims traveled during the first centuries of the Christian epoch to India, to bring the teachings and conclusions of the Buddha back to their own country. Indian scholars were also invited to visit the Middle Empire, and some of them taught there. If account is taken of the difficulties of crossing the Himalayas, which were certainly greater then than now, it is astonishing what a vigorous cultural exchange developed between the two countries. The Himalayas constituted no barrier between them, but merely an obstacle that was surmounted by faith.

The first Buddhist community in China was founded A.D. 60 or 70, and 250 years later there were some 180 Buddhist settlements and 3,700 monks in the two towns Changan and Loyang alone. Hundreds of Buddhist works were translated into Chinese, and monks set out on the perilous road to India solely "to buy books."

The best known of the Chinese pilgrims were Fa-Hsien, Sung Yung, Hsüan Tsang, and I Tsing. They described their journeys with a characteristically Chinese love of detail, and their books were read with the same interest as were those of Marco Polo and Sven Hedin in later centuries. The latter moreover confirms that the old Chinese descriptions and maps were the mainstay of his first travels in Tibet. They were in fact Baedekers for hundreds of years.

These accounts were colorful enough; thus Wang Huen Tse, who traveled in the days of the T'ang Dynasty (618–907), describes the King of Nepal as follows: "He wears real pearls, diamonds, coral and amber, and he sits on a throne decorated with lions, amid a fragrance of flowers and perfumes. In the midst of the palace rises a seven-storied tower with roofs of copper."

Hsüan Tsang writes of Nepal: "The territory of Ni-Po-Lo lies in the midst of the snow mountains. The earth is rich in flowers and fruits, the climate cool. The inhabitants are rude and of a wild nature. They are interested neither in the true faith nor in justice nor literature, but are good crafts-men and artists. Their houses are of wood, carved and painted. They enjoy taking baths. They love drama, astrology and bloody sacrifices."

The dangers of the mountains were the same then as now: "...overhanging cliffs, peaks towering to heaven... the most outstanding of our famous mountains [in China] are like level country... when one looks into the depths it is as though one were floating unsupported in space. Men say that this is the point midway between heaven and earth..."

The mountaineers of our own day have found no finer words to express the impact of this high-altitude world. For the Chinese, however, the mountains were not the object of the journey but an irksome and dangerous obstacle on the way of truth. They never saw the beauty of the high peaks, but only their terrors.

The next explorers of the Himalayas did not come until several centuries later, and they too were motivated by religious faith. They were the Christian missionaries, setting out to convert the Orient to their teachings. They were preceded by Marco Polo, known as *Il Milione*, partly because he estimated the riches of the East in terms of millions, partly because his accounts of his travels seemed to his contemporaries to be a million lies. Today they are included among the literary treasures of the world. He told of magicians at the court of Kublai Khan who demonstrated the power of their gods by means of "flying trays" loaded with golden dishes and goblets which they caused to float through the hall, bringing refreshment to the Great Khan. His descriptions sound like fairy tales, but they are certainly his genuine experience. It was also he who first noticed something that has caused later mountaineers a deal of trouble—namely, at great altitudes a fire does not give "the same heat" as in the valleys, and that it is hard to get food adequately cooked.

The China trade which Marco Polo initiated generally followed the silk route, avoiding the high mountains. But the Christian missionaries—men whose courage in their faith, as well as their knowledge and determination, was astounding—tried to set up the kingdom of God on the high plains of Tibet and among the snow mountains of the Himalayas.

The first European to reach Lhasa was the Franciscan Oderico of Pordenone (1286–1331) from Friuli in northern Italy. He died shortly before reaching Europe on his return journey, and his report found little credence. Its reliability is still often questioned.

In 1624 Antonio de Andrada was permitted to found a mission in Tsaparang (southern Tibet), although the brother of the local king was the chief of the lama priests. He crossed the Mana Pass (18,000 feet) during the monsoon and describes how in the breast-high snow he lost a finger through frostbite without feeling the slightest pain: "I would not have believed it if I had not seen the blood flow. Our feet were frozen and swollen..." Probably he was the first European to look down from the Himalayas onto the uplands of Tibet: "It was all one dazzling whiteness before our eyes, which were already weakened by snow blindness. We could see no trace of a path to follow..." In Tsaparang he built a Christian church. The edict of the Tibetan king ran: "...let him be given every opportunity to instruct our people in the Holy Law... he is to be given land and every assistance in the building of a house of prayer."

The generosity with which the Oriental rulers of those days received and examined a strange faith seems extraordinary today. Communist Tibet, having expelled its last missionaries, is now closed to all Western influence, and even the independent kingdom of Nepal has forbidden them all pastoral activity. But in the seventeenth and early eighteenth centuries Tibet and Nepal were favored missions. The Jesuits had won themselves a respected position at the court of Peking, and they frequently visited the Himalayas on their way back to Europe by land.

Father Johannes Grueber (1623–80) from Linz in Austria lived for years at the Manchu court as an official of the imperial observatory. When he was ordered home, the sea route being blocked by the Dutch navy, he was given permission to travel "by land." He stayed six weeks in Lhasa, where he was the first to make a drawing of the Potala, the fortified monastery of the Dalai Lama, the construction of which had been started a few years earlier. In the winter he reached Katmandu.

One of the greatest personalities of the epoch was Hippolytus Desideri (1684–1753). He was sent to reopen the mission founded by Andrada at Tsaparang and traveled via Kashmir to Lhasa, where he lived and taught for seven years. But he did more than teach; he learned the Tibetan language

Lama with a conch. Drawing by Sven Hedin.
(From Sven Hedin, *Transhimalaya*, Leipzig, 1909)

and script and studied the 108 volumes of the Kanjur, the sacred book of Tibet. He wrote a book in Tibetan refuting the doctrine of soul migration, which could not be reconciled with Christian teaching. He discussed with the lamas the most difficult questions arising from the two religions. Moreover, he was an acute observer who described many particulars of the land and people without exaggerating. Sven Hedin called him "one of the most magnificent and brilliant travelers who ever visited Tibet, and among the oldest of them the most eminent and most gifted."

The rulers of China also—like Mao Tse-tung today—took an interest in Tibet, and the Emperor K'ang-li sent out Buddhist monks to make a geographical survey of the country. They were instructed in trigonometry by the Jesuits in Peking, and their maps found their way to Europe, where Jean Baptiste Bourgignon d'Anville made use of them in his great work in 1783.

However the information thus gained about the distant uplands and mountains was soon forgotten again in Europe, and it was not until England and Russia confronted each other mistrustfully on the high passes of Asia that the Himalayas reappeared in the field of view of the West.

No people has deified its mountains or seen them as the scene of divine events to the same extent as the Indians. Material causes may have contributed to this.

Even for the mountaineer with modern equipment the Himalayas are forbidding; for the Indians of bygone centuries, coming from their scorching plains, they must have been another and an inaccessible world—heaven itself, in fact, the dispenser of life. For the monsoon rains were but a transient gift; during the dry season it was the great rivers from the Himalayas that brought the precious water that meant life. For the believing Hindu the entire Himalayas are identical with the god Shiva: The chief east-west chains are the god's brows, the formations running south his locks. The monk and the widow cut off their hair in token of world abnegation or of mourning; death is hairless; how much life must there be in the Himalayas then, for the glory of their hair to reach the heavens!

The Himalayas are mentioned in the oldest of Indian writings, appearing in the Vedas as Devabhumi, or land of the gods, the area in which the Ganges rises being Devatatma, or home of the gods. The sources of the Ganges are still to this day the favorite goal of pilgrims, who feel that there they can pay their respects to the gods in their private home.

There is no need to seek long in the writings of Hinduism to find words in praise of the Himalayas.

According to a Sanscrit proverb, "A hundred divine epochs would not suffice to describe all the marvels of the Himalayas."

"Where shall he who has seen the marvels of the Himalayas find fitting words of praise for the Creator?" asks Hindu piety.

In the days when the epic poems *Ramayana* and *Mahabharata* originated, the southern slopes of the Himalayas were already known, for the gods of the Himalayas called, and the devout went as pilgrims to the heights.

The Indian poet Kalidasa (perhaps fifth century A.D.), whom Goethe called one of the great masters in the literature of the world, reveals astonishing geographical knowledge in his masterpiece "The Cloud Messenger" (*Meghaduta*). A captive in India sends his beloved, who lives near Mount Kailas in the Himalayas, a message of love, using for the purpose a cloud which is setting out on the long journey over the mountains. The poem contains exact descriptions of the course of the valleys and the beauties and difficulties of the waterfalls and displays a profound knowledge of the nature of the Himalayas. Since it is unlikely that Kalidasa had himself undertaken the pilgrimage to Mount Kailas, he must have used the accounts of other travelers. It is evident that the Himalayas were "explored" from the south at a very early date.

But in "The Cloud Messenger" the geographical facts are unimportant by comparison with the beauty of the poetry:

> The Himalayan winds that plunder many a flower
> And hasten, nectar-sweet, onward toward the south,
> Cool my hot breast, delighting with the thought
> That once, perhaps, not long ago they touched thy limbs.

It was not only the Hindus who saw the Himalayas as a dwelling place of the gods, for Indian Moslems also regarded them as sacred. The Emperor Akbar (the Great—1542–1605) sent an expedition to explore the sources of the Ganges, and his geographers produced a map in which the Brahmaputra and the Sutlej originate in Manasarowar Lake.

Moslems in later ages also gave expression to their reverence for the Himalayas. The great poet Mohammed Iqbal (1873–1938)—one of the heralds of the Pakistan of today—dreamed of an Islamic empire with the Himalayas as its northern defense barrier:

> O Himalayas, strong rampart of the Indian realm!
> The heavens bend down to kiss your brow.

15 Figure of the god Vishnu, known in Nepal as Narayan, on a bed of serpents. The king may not visit this shrine, for he is himself held to be an incarnation of the god. Near Katmandu

The Land of Holy Men

I owe my acquaintance and occasional friendships with the holy men of the Himalayas to chance and impecuniousness. As a young student I was collecting materials in Kashmir for my doctoral thesis in geology, and when the summer came, my wanderlust overcoming my scientific zeal, I decided to make the pilgrimage to the Cave of Amarnath. Situated at an altitude of nearly 13,000 feet among the magnificent mountains of Kashmir, it is sacred to Shiva the Destroyer and a goal that every pious Hindu longs to reach. The pilgrims from hot India, unaccustomed to altitude, cold, and snow, make complicated and old-fashioned preparations for this trip.

I believed that I knew mountains and could do it more simply. I was accompanied by an Indian student, Chatter Kapur, who subsequently went with me to Tibet. We packed some provisions and our sleeping bags in rucksacks and set out. No doubt we dawdled on our march, but as long as we met other pilgrims, there was much to see and hear. We came to a lake with ice-cold glacier water, inhabited, so the legend claims, by a thousand-headed serpent, well disposed toward pilgrims. It is said that once it killed a demon who had taken on the form of a storm with intent to exterminate the faithful, who have shown their gratitude ever since by washing in the waters of the lake—after prudently warming them first.

When we reached our destination a few days later, all the pilgrims were gone, for the auspicious days for the sacrifice were past—and our provisions were finished. The cave, into which the rays of the sun never penetrate, is full of ice. Water drips from the roof, forming upward-pointing stalagmites, reminiscent of the lingam, the fertility symbol of Hinduism, and revered by the pilgrims as sacred.

When our eyes had grown accustomed to the gloom, we saw a sadhu sitting in the background, only lightly clothed despite the cold and enveloped in his long hair and white beard. We touched his feet in the proper manner, and a friendly conversation soon developed.

The pilgrims had left many nutritious offerings, and the holy man did not seem to be in want. Our destitute rucksacks amused him highly, and he said it was a topsy-turvy world in which instead of our bringing him offerings, he had to provide for us. This he did with such disarming amiability that we felt no embarrassment. After resting for a day, we took our leave, he pressing juicy apples and stale chapati bread on us and giving us his blessing when we left. That was my first—rather unconventional—meeting with a hermit.

In the college at Srinagar I had a tiny room, or rather cell, furnished solely with a table, a chair, and a wooden bed. There was no necessity to lock doors, and it was not customary to do so. One day, some weeks after the excursion to Amarnath, on returning from some geological work that had kept me away for some time, I found an intruder in my room. He reminded me of the hermit of Amarnath and was sitting in the posture of the Buddha on the mud floor in meditation. Some hours later his spirit returned, and he informed me as though it were a matter of course that he was going to stay with me for a while. When in some embarrassment I drew his attention to the simplicity of my lodging, he replied with a deprecating smile that he was not accustomed to luxury. After so shamelessly taking advantage of the hospitality of the holy man at Amarnath, I was only too glad to be able to make some return to a colleague of his. Our life together was strange. Sometimes he left me for considerable periods to meditate and teach under a shady tree. He must have been a man of distinction, for my room became a center of worship. We—I cannot avoid the "we"— received more offerings than even I with my student's appetite could get through. The local dignitaries—even the Srinagar police, who had not hitherto looked with particular favor on either me or my motorcycle—became friendly and obliging. It was the zenith of my social career during all my time in India.

I never discovered why this holy man chose to honor me with his favor. Had he perhaps heard of our unpilgrimly behavior at the cave and been amused by it? Or did he see in me a possible disciple? He told me that he was bound for the sacred town of Muktinath in Nepal, and if I wished I might accompany him. It was 1935, and Nepal still forbidden territory, so I was afire to go. A permit from the maharaja would be required, but my sadhu was acquainted with the monarch and would see to that. We composed a courteous application and soon afterward received a reply. It was in correct English, short and disappointing: "Dear Sir, His Highness has found it inconvenient to give you permission."

That put an end to my dream of a journey to Nepal. The holy man proceeded on his way just as he had arrived, simply as a matter of course. He comforted me in my disappointment: "You will see Muktinath too one day. I know it."

I had not yet learned that especial importance should be attached to the words of a sadhu, but a few years later, when I really was in Muktinath, I thought of the prophecy of my friend in Kashmir. I never saw him or heard of him again.

In the eyes of devout Hindus I am perhaps a thoroughly meritorious pilgrim, for I have visited many of their holy places. I have made the circuit of "the most holy mountain in the world," Kailas, and washed away my sins in "the most harmonious lake in the world," Manasarowar. In Badrinath, Kedarmath, Yoshimath, and other places of pilgrimage I have been for weeks together a familiar, if not welcome, figure in the temples. I was engaged at the time by a German illustrated magazine, whose editors I had persuaded that I could get photographs of the fabulous miracles of the "Masters," such as levitation.

I told them a story that I had often heard in the Himalayas, of how a mountaineer, reaching the highest village below the eternal snow, saw there a half-naked yogi, attired only in rags. He made mild fun of him, saying that he could hardly expect to climb far with such equipment and asking whether he was not afraid of getting frostbite in his toes. But when the mountaineer, after indescribable exertions and with the help of porters and guides, at last scaled the summit, he found the yogi sitting there, praying. "Did you really come up here on foot?" asked the latter. I never succeeded in seeing a "flying lama," but I have met many charlatans and a few great holy men.

Since Indians in general find pilgrimages in the Himalayas onerous, it is sometimes possible to impress them with accounts of one's own pious expeditions. Once I even achieved a great success

16 The holy man of Badrinath, who has been meditating in the Himalayas for ten years

17 The begging bowl of a sadhu placed near a pilgrims' path

18 One of the lingamlike natural formations on a glacier near Helmkund. These are worshiped by pilgrims like the one whose arms are seen here

19 Mount Kailas, "the holiest mountain in the world" and the living place of Shiva, is revered by Buddhists and Hindus

20 Rock face with the incised prayer *O mani padme hum*

21 Figure carved in wood, Kafiristan

22 Cemetery in Kafiristan. The strongly made coffins are not buried. The figures are memorials to persons of merit

23 Lamas in the monastery of Kumbum praying before a wrought-iron grille behind which are statues of the Buddha

24 Lamas in Kumbum preparing to put themselves into a state of trance by gazing fixedly at brass bowls filled with water

25 Indian pilgrim at a rest hut. He is viewing the glacier-covered peaks that are the throne of his gods

26 A chorten or Lamaist monument, in the village of Banphag, northern Nepal

in this way. It was in the Bombay Customs Office, after I had climbed the 26,000-foot peak of Cho Oyu.

On entering India a list of all articles imported must be submitted, and on leaving they all must be produced for reexport. Now we had brought with us, for ourselves, our Sherpas and the other porters, 180 pairs of woolen socks and stockings. After three months nothing much was left of these but holes, apart from those that had perhaps landed in some Sherpa household. In any case we presented ourselves with only a negligible number of these articles in hand. Our hint that the counting of socks that had been worn for months would not be an enjoyable occupation either for the customs officer or ourselves fell on deaf ears, reinforced by smell-hardened noses: We were liable for duty. I tried a macabre joke, pointing out that I had imported ten living fingers, but now, after frostbite, I had only nine and a half to show; must I pay duty on the missing joints? The official produced a list of dutiable articles twice the size of the telephone directory of a large town and began to consult one page after another with enervating thoroughness. Finally, he produced the official answer: "No, portions of the human anatomy are not subject to duty."

I was on the point of giving in when I remembered Mount Kailas. Each of us, I told him, had worn through four pairs of socks on the pilgrimage there; practically nothing had been left of them, for the way is long and arduous, but the end repays every effort. I had no need of much exaggeration to rouse myself to enthusiasm, and since I had recently written an article on Kailas, I was even able to quote a few lines from the *Ramayana* epic: "If the earth of the Manasarowar district touches any man's body, or if he bathes in the lake, that man shall go to the paradise of Brahma, or he who drinks its waters shall know the heaven of Shiva. Nowhere are there mountains equal to the Himalayas, for in them are both Kailas and Manasarowar."

I gazed reproachfully at the customs officer. I had earned a double paradise, and here was he plaguing me in his stuffy office. His eyes grew moist with sentiment, and the wretched socks were finally forgotten. One might call it bribery by religion.

On the return march from Mount Kailas we really did have hardly any socks left, and our legs were covered with wounds and sores. This caused us no little embarrassment. As I shall recount later, I had gone to Tibet in defiance of the prohibition of the Indian government, using the disguise

16

21

22

of a pilgrim. We had departed early in the year, and as we made our way through the narrow valleys back to India, we were quite rightly accounted the first pilgrims of the season and were welcomed accordingly. The local people hung sweet-smelling garlands around our necks, gave us sticky sweetmeats to eat, and were particularly moved to pity by our bleeding feet, which they washed, anointed, and pressed to their foreheads—all things which it is pleasanter to read about in the Bible than to have actually done to one. Moreover, we were apprehensive lest my disguise, which had survived every suspicious glance hitherto, should now be penetrated. My black hair dye had run out, and my head displayed strange contrasts in color, but we reached India without any trouble.

But the Indian Security Service was more vigilant than we had supposed. Shortly after I had resumed my studies at the University of Lahore, I received a letter from the governor of the Punjab, informing me that he had learned of my escapade and envied me the experience. In younger days an official mission had taken him to Mount Kailas, so he knew the sublime quality of the scenery and congratulated me on having seen it all. At the same time he had to inform me that in the course of the next few days he would have me arrested for illegally crossing the frontier.

I took the friendly hint, mounted my motorcycle, and returned to Europe via Afghanistan. A few years later, when he had retired, I was able to thank him personally for his magnanimity, but he answered with a smile that one Kailas pilgrim would surely not arrest another.

The great mountaineering expeditions rarely report meetings with hermits and holy men; that is probably because they are too numerous and have a specific goal, toward which they press noisily forward. The hermits, as befits their vocation, love solitude and quiet.

Near Badrinath I met the holy man, or sadhu, who is shown in the second illustration in this volume. He dwelled in a tiny stone shelter, almost naked and apparently insensitive to cold, for it was autumn, and the temperature sank to below freezing at night. I never saw him eat. The inhabitants of Badrinath, who moved south in November, told me that he had once spent a bitterly cold winter there alone and without provisions. When I asked him if he needed no nourishment and how such a way of life was medically possible, he replied with a counter-question: "Have you heard of Thérèse of Konnersreuth? And have you in Europe any explanation for that?"

Once we discussed the widespread legend that Jesus had spent part of his life in a Buddhist monastery, having come at the age of fourteen to Hemis Gompa, the first monastery to be set up in Ladakh, not returning to the West until he was twenty-eight. I asked what the sadhu thought of this.

"Are facts, space, and time so important?" he answered. "Jesus existed, and we revere him."

He made no objection to my passing many hours near him. He was generally in the state of meditation, in which no doubt he did not notice my presence, but a feeling of peace, stillness, and sublimity emanated from him, such as may be felt in the silence of a cathedral. He was an educated man who had studied jurisprudence in England, had held office as a judge in India, and had founded a family. Then he received the "call," and when I met him, he had been living for ten years in the Himalayas.

In contrast with the charlatans who perform tricks of hypnosis and display bodily feats for alms on the pilgrim routes, he was really far advanced in the art of yoga. The word "yoga" comes from the Sanskrit *yuj*, to connect or unite. It is only by uniting the personal ego with the essence of things, or the world soul, or God, that truth can be directly experienced. That which the mystics of Europe achieve only in moments of ecstasy is here reduced to an almost scientifically cool-headed system of breath control and concentration. When I asked the sadhu to be my guru or teacher, he gave the expected answer: He was an unworthy guru, for he had not yet reached the end of his way, and I was not yet a worthy disciple. I should wait; perhaps in a year or two. Time was no object; like everything here, it was relative. Nothing must be hurried, and humility was indispensable.

How could I, who loved not only the peace of meditation but also the fight with the mountains, who could not free myself of worldly desires—how could I be a good disciple?

Other pilgrims achieved no such perfection, being content to look upon the throne of the gods and to free themselves of some of their sins. The Himalayas with their shining white peaks are the symbol of purity for them, and an old Hindu proverb says, "The sight of the snows wipes out the sins of the world." Even in the days of the Vedas the inhabitants of India were enjoined to go on pilgrimage: "There is no happiness for him who does not travel. Even the best of men, if he lives among others, often becomes a sinner. Indra is a friend of travelers; therefore travel!" One of the oldest chants, or puranas, has the following effusion: "A hundred lives are not enough to tell of the glories of the Himachal. As the dew before the sun, so does everything base vanish away at the sight of the eternally pure Home of the Snow."

Therefore, hundreds are on the march, and the Himalayas have become a "social safety valve" for India, where not only the true seekers of God, but also the eccentrics, the unhappy, the heavy-laden, the weary and the branded all seek peace.

Katmandu, the capital of Nepal, a dozen years ago unknown and hardly visited by Europeans but later embraced by Cook's round-the-world trips and development aid, has become a paradise of the international layabouts and hippies. It is certainly not only the beauty of the town, the agreeable climate, and the cheerful friendliness of the inhabitants that exert this attraction, but also the magic of the Himalayas and the largeheartedness of the various religions, which intermingle here on friendly terms, seeming to invite an international "love-in."

I encountered some truly strange figures on my travels. There was for instance a sadhu who had crawled from South India to the source of the Ganges. He had taken eight years to do it. He did not really crawl, but measured out the way with the length of his body, throwing himself flat on the ground and then repeating the process from the spot reached by his fingers. But to avoid allowing his pilgrimage to become too easy or too quick, he turned around after every three prostrations and made the fourth backward. This form of penance was extensively practiced in Tibet, and the pilgrims would make the circuit of Mount Kailas in this way over cliffs and glaciers on the icy heights. Normally it takes two days, but for them two months. They generally wear gloves with soles like shoes, and often they have a thick layer of calloused skin on the forehead, with which they touch the ground.

Pande, with whom I made friends and in whose company for several weeks I "looked for God," as he rather ironically called it, was a very different type. He came from Bombay and was a restless person, who in his youth had joined first a radical organization on the extreme right and then the

46

Mani-stones. (From Joseph Dalton Hooker,
Himalayan Journal, London, 1855)

Communist Party. Then for a while he found peace in marriage, three children, and a business, but his entire family died within a week in a cholera epidemic. So he had come to the Himalayas "to give God one last chance." He was no quiet, humble seeker of God who could wait for grace like the yogis; he wanted a quick decision. During long evenings and long nights he proved himself a choice partner in discussions in which he quoted thinkers as different as Marx, Huxley, Koestler, and Nehru with amazing familiarity. The simple pilgrims with their peasant faith he regarded with scorn, ridiculing the strange forms of their worship.

But once, in the vicinity of the sacred lake of Helmkund—in the neighborhood of Badrinath the majority of landmarks count as sacred—when we came upon some pilgrims worshiping a glacier, he did not want me to photograph them. He said this was something typically Indian, and people in Europe would misunderstand it. In fact the pilgrims were not worshiping the glacier itself, but only its special conformations, for the wind had blown hay from the surrounding fields onto the ice, and here the sun had melted out pyramidal cones resembling the glacier tables. These spooky images had found worshipers who saw in them symbols of the power of generation and creation. The chauvinist had raised his head in Pande, who was otherwise ready to mock at everything. I do not know what has become of him; perhaps he is leader of a Communist cell in Kerala, or perhaps he is sitting cross-legged in a cave in the Himalayas, seeking his way or at the end of it.

When I think of the "holy" Himalayas, it is not only the people who are seeking their God there that I see and hear; I also remember the sacred objects connected with their worship. For instance the chortens, chapellike buildings or high cairns on which every wayfarer who has successfully negotiated the difficulties of the path lays a stone. Particularly pious or superstitious leaders of caravans were not content with that but used to scatter rice, flour, and small pieces of butter into the wind as thank offerings to the gods. And then there are the countless mani-stones, sometimes no larger than roofing tiles, sometimes huge rock faces on which the faithful, or craftsmen paid by them, have chiseled the ancient prayer "O Jewel in the Lotus Flower." Or again the prayer walls, some no longer than the side of a house, but others hundreds of yards in length, running as straight as a die through an uninhabited countryside. They may be passed only on the left, so as the track approaches one of them, it divides into two, embracing it like two arms raised in prayer. And an unforgettable feature are the larger chortens, from which the eyes of the Buddha gaze out, peaceful and all-knowing, over the land. A kind of dialogue takes place as one approaches these eyes, for they are kindly, but their omniscience is disconcerting. No good denying that we have sinned and gone astray, for the Buddha knows it. But are we mistaken, or do the eyes seem to smile? Have we found forgiveness?

The sacred buildings and religious symbols do not everywhere possess the clearly intelligible beauty of the "eyes of Buddha." In the central Himalayas, where the Lamaism penetrating from the north mingles with the Hinduism of the south, the people seeking salvation in both, the measures taken against demons and evil spirits are often hard to interpret. In metropolitan Katmandu, where the best artists and most learned priests reside, the expert can interpret every statue and every painting but in the isolated valleys with their primitive populations one is apt to be confronted by an enigma.

In Bangthari, a tiny village in Nepal, for instance, I felt as though I had found my way into an exhibition of modern art. The outer walls of the houses were painted with spirals, circles, crosses, and a variety of forms in which fantasy ran riot. The colors were carefully chosen, neither glaring nor monotonous. When I asked the reason for this artistic activity, I was informed that painting drove off evil spirits. There was no artist or priest to execute these murals; every householder painted his own. I reflected that Picasso was lucky not to live in Bangthari, for he would hardly have been noticed there.

Nowhere else did I find the beautiful spirals of Bangthari, for the surrounding villages put their trust in sculpture, rather than painting. The carvings, however, confirmed that the inhabitants of this district, which is that surrounding Tibrikot in West Nepal, are endowed with exceptional talent and fantasy. They are neither Hindus nor Buddhists, having their own gods, called Masta. These deities are watched over by guards carved in wood in the form of grotesque human bodies or masks; they are called Dok-pa, are protectors against all kinds of evil, and often outnumber the human inhabitants. They keep watch everywhere—before the houses, at the wells, on the fields, along the paths—and if they could be relied on, the inhabitants of Tibrikot would lead a carefree life.

The Himalayan monasteries are hospitable, giving shelter even to "unbelievers." The lamas, despite their dignity and the pomp that surrounds them, are childlike and at the same time full of interest for the world. They are highly artistic, and the famous dances they perform on festive occasions are orgies of color and demonstrations of the science of movement in which gods, demons, and human beings act out the drama of life and that of the remote myths. The interiors of the temples are mostly gloomy, and it is only when the eyes have grown accustomed to the half-light that details can be distinguished. Then it is seen that the decorations are not confined to the usual peaceful Buddha statues, but also include threatening grotesque masks and many-headed gods of death, trampling on human bodies. But all are symbols of the universal Deity, and beside them stands

27 The Newaris,
now no longer
a political power, once adorned
the Katmandu Valley
with innumerable magnificent
works of art

a prayer wheel, waiting for a pious hand to turn it and thereby add the petitions inscribed on it to those which the wind has received from the prayer flags and swept up to heaven.

In Yoshimath the Sherpa Nima and I fought a cheerful but obstinately contested battle with the aged priest Govindanand. For several weeks we had shared the Spartan life of the hermits, eating neither vegetables nor fruit, and we craved vitamins. The bazaar at Yoshimath could supply only onions and garlic, but with these we were content. When the appetizing savor of the rice with onions which Nima had prepared spread through the building, however, Govindanand burst into our cell in a rage. Did we not know, he asked, that onions were an "apple of voluptuousness," strictly forbidden in the monastery?

No, we did not know it, and we had no voluptuous desires whatever. Hostilities ensued, ending with our eating the onions, which we really did not want to forgo, raw and at a safe distance from the monastery, although this did not diminish the sinful smell that emanated from us. Nevertheless, we departed in peace and with the priest's blessing. In allusion to my mountaineering aspirations he gave me a magnificent parable as a parting gift. "You seek the sun," he said, "and before you

Mural painting on the exterior of the Ri-bo-Khang Temple (From L. Jisl, V. Sís, J. Vaniš, *Tibetische Kunst*, Prague, 1958)

50

there are a couple of bowls of water. You are accustomed to direct your gaze downward, so all you see is the miserable reflection. You clutch the bowls and believe you have captured the sun."

A few years previously I had seen the lamas of Kumbum gazing at just such bowls and passing into the state of meditation. It was after World War II, and I wanted to travel overland from China to India, but since everything was in a state of confusion and I had no passport, I remained stuck at the frontier between China and Tibet, in the monastery of Kumbum, which means "ten thousand pictures." I was not allowed to go farther, and in the end I had to return to Peking "as the guest of two soldiers," as Chinese politeness described it.

But while I was waiting, Kumbum received me with a warmth I shall never forget. I was by no means a desirable guest, for I was not in favor with the Chinese authorities, with whom the lamas were on none too good terms either. Nevertheless, I found a home there. In Sining, not far away, Catholic and Protestant missionaries—the only Europeans far and wide—lived side by side without speaking, but in Kumbum there were no barriers, either of religion or of race. When I left, the lamas called after me "Come again—we are your father and your mother!" That was no empty phrase, for they had put it to the proof. When I think of the monks of Kumbum, I have the same feelings as I have about the holy men of the Himalayas: love, warmth, and the longing to become a little like them.

Spies Who Went into the Cold

In the course of thousands of years great empires arose and disappeared again and again both north and south of the Himalayas. The subcontinent of India brought forth civilizations at a high level of culture, destined at last to be submerged by the desert sands or the inroads of barbarians. In the Central Asian steppes Huns, Tatars, and Mongols built up their forces and then attempted to impose their rule on the known world of their day. The crucial point is that the fate of Asia was always decided by Asians; there was only Alexander's brief campaign to leave its traces of European art and philosophy. Europe, apart from the influence of the traveling missionaries and merchants, was as remote for Asians as Cathay was for Europeans.

But in time Europe began to reach out for Asia—first with the cross, then with the sword, and finally with trade, as Asians are apt to complain. Russia enlarged her sphere of influence southward in the main continental landmass, while Britain established herself in India. The British lion and the Russian bear, a safe distance apart in Europe, confronted each other on the passes of the Pamirs, the Karakorum, and the Himalayas, each watching the doings of the other with a suspicious eye.

The "great game for Asia," which Rudyard Kipling describes with so much color and but little exaggeration in *Kim*, had begun. This game was in reality nothing but a precursor of our cold war, fought with threats and chessboard moves similar to those in use today. More important than armaments were the secrets of the unknown region that lay between the antagonists. The spies of those days were the explorers, for their discoveries not only served to satisfy the thirst for know-

28 Shrine in the Buddhist monastery Swayambunath, near Katmandu, one of the oldest sacred places in Nepal. Tame holy monkeys live among the statues of the gods
29 A chorten in the Barbung Khola, northern Nepal, looking south. In the background is Dhaulagiri
30 A chorten in Nepal
31 "The omniscient eyes of Buddha"
32 Evening falls on a village in Nepal

33 Giant prayer wheel in a lama temple
34 Interior of a lama temple, with its pantheon of gods and demons
35, 36, 38 and 39 Lama dancers in their brilliantly colored costumes and fantastic masks
37 Deity in a lama temple
40 Reincarnation of a high lama in the Boddhnath temple near Katmandu

ledge of the scholars and the curiosity of the public, but also provided the military staffs with the information they needed for their planning. It is easy to understand the mistrust with which Britain followed the great journeys of Sven Hedin, and likewise to comprehend the assertion made by Chou En-lai in Katmandu that every Himalaya expedition carried on espionage. In a way he is right, for the skirmishes between India and China have shown that the Himalayas have long ceased to be an impassable frontier defense and that every geographical or meteorological discovery has its military value.

In the middle of the nineteenth century the British, having conquered the rich land of India, pressed their explorations to the confines of those territories whose rulers tolerated white men. Nepal, Bhutan, and Tibet closed their frontiers, and Chinese Turkistan was still in the throes of the Tungan rebellion, so that access to all those blank spaces on the map which might become threats to India was cut off.

The Indian Survey thereupon devised the expedient of training Indians, mostly inhabitants of the Himalayas and thus accustomed to mountains, in the elements of surveying and sending them out with specific geographical assignments on their adventurous journeys. Because these men belonged largely, although not exclusively, to the priestly caste, they were known as pundits, and under this name they hold a place of honor in the history of exploration. Their true names are hardly known, for they appear in the archives as mysterious code letters and numbers. Thus there was a No. 1, as well as A-K, D-C-S, G-M-N, and the modest L, all of which codes hide the identity of "spies who went into the cold" in search of the geographical secrets of the Himalayas and Tibet. They disguised themselves as pilgrims, merchants, or monks, or they acquired a few medical techniques; in short, they managed to move freely on the dangerous paths of inner Asia. The observations which they surreptitiously secured they inscribed on the paper strip of a prayer wheel, and they kept count of their steps with the aid of a rosary.

Nain Singh, who reached Lhasa, made observations over a route of 1,250 miles in South Tibet, and followed the course of the Tsangpo for 600 miles, was acclaimed by his learned British colleagues as "one who has supplied more positive information to the cartographers than any other man living." He was known as No. 1 or simply Pundit.

His cousin Kishen Singh became famous as A-K, whose most important journey lasted four years, taking him from Darjeeling via Lhasa to Mongolia and Northwest China. When all hope of

52

29

30

31

32

37

38

39

his return had been abandoned, he reappeared with a vast quantity of geographical information the accuracy of which was still arousing the admiration of European explorers decades later.

The most adventurous of all these pundit journeys had the purpose of solving the riddle of the Brahmaputra. At that time opinions differed on whether the Tsangpo, which flows eastward from Mount Kailas across Tibet, was identical with the mighty Brahmaputra, which reaches Assam through the Himalayan gorges. The officials of the survey believed that it was, but the experts in Europe demanded proof. A Chinese lama, resident in Darjeeling, was chosen to decide the issue. After undergoing suitable training, he was to be sent out to follow the course of the Tsangpo and throw marked pieces of wood into the stream, while in Assam a careful watch was to be kept on the Brahmaputra for them. The lama was supplied with an uneducated servant named Kinthup to alleviate the hardships of the journey, but when he reached Lhasa, his love of gain overbore his enthusiasm for discovery: He sold Kinthup into slavery and himself disappeared from the annals of exploration. The slave Kinthup on the other hand holds a place of honor in those annals, and years later he was to be publicly decorated by the viceroy of India. But before he reached that point, he had to undergo many exciting experiences and accept many disappointments. He succeeded in escaping from slavery, and by working as a tailor—a tailor in Tibet!—he even put some money by. Then he completed the assignment abandoned by his Chinese master: He threw the wooden markers into the Tsangpo, the course of which he followed to within 30 miles of the frontier of Assam. Finding no way through the wild gorges, he returned to India by another route.

In the meanwhile, the survey people had vainly kept watch on the Brahmaputra, seeking the wooden markers, for two years; then, with the death of Captain Harman, who had been in charge of the project, the whole matter was forgotten.

Four years had passed since the departure of the lama when Kinthup found his way back with his report. But Harman was dead, the Brahmaputra problem forgotten, and Kinthup nothing but a ragged, half-starved native. He had to wait two years before he could tell his story.

When he did tell it, the white sahibs could not believe it. Kinthup was not trained as a surveyor and could not even read or write. But with the aid of a photographic memory he was able to describe every curve of the Tsangpo and every peculiarity of the landscape, so that the map based on his account was later found to be astonishingly accurate. Outside survey circles, doubts were cast on it, but the Anglo-Indian officials believed Kinthup "because he had described the colors in the rainbow at the foot of a great waterfall in exact detail." Twenty years later H. T. Morshead and S. M. Bailey explored the gorges of the Tsangpo and confirmed Kinthup's description of them, so that the latter, long forgotten, was granted his triumph in his old age: He was invited to Simla and received by the viceroy, who bestowed honors and presents on him.

With this episode, toward the end of last century, the adventurous times of the pundits come to an end, and the first mountaineers appear in the Himalayas: men who were pursuing neither scientific nor military ends, but simply wanted to climb a high peak.

The "Unbelievers"

"In his wanderings among the mountains a man came upon the palace of the fairies of Nanga Parbat. It was built of shining crystal, and in the middle of the garden stood a tree with pearls hanging from its branches. The man picked them, stowed them in a sack, and was just making off when he saw that he was being followed by snakes. Overcome by fear, he threw away the pearls, which the snakes swallowed and then disappeared. The man reached home safely, but four days later he died, for the fairies never forgive those who discover their secrets."

This symbolic tale of the "killer mountain" is told by the Kafirs, who do not belong to the Himalayan peoples in the strict sense. There are only from 3,000 to 4,000 of them, and they live in the three valleys of Rumbur, Brumburet, and Birir, which lead from Chitral to the Afghan frontier. Just as the Gurkhas owe their renown to their bravery, and the Sherpas theirs to their faithfulness, so have the Kafirs become known on account of their origins or, to be precise, the scientific uncertainty regarding their origins.

"Kafir" means unbeliever, and the Kafirs accepted this somewhat contemptuous name from the Moslems. They do not constitute an organized people, but simply a group united in opposition to Islam. They regard Europeans also as their brothers not because they suppose a common origin, but because both are non-Moslems.

The Kafirs are tall and sometimes blond and blue-eyed. They were long held to be the descendants of groups cut off from Alexander the Great's army, but fair-haired inhabitants of the Hindu Kush were already known to the historians of ancient Greece. According to another theory, they are descended from the Varangians. Perhaps they sprang from the stock of the white Huns or the Kushan.

The Kafirs themselves assert on occasion that they are emigrants from Arabia who belonged to the tribes from which the Prophet sprang but rejected his religion and sought a new home.

They also tell the following legend: God divided the earth among the peoples, giving the desert to the Arabs and the jungle to the Negroes, but keeping the most beautiful place on earth for himself, namely the valleys of Kafiristan. When it was discovered that the Kafirs had been left out, and they remonstrated, he in his infinite goodness gave them their present home.

That home is surrounded by adversaries and is steadily shrinking. The part that lies in Afghanistan was bloodily converted to Islam by Abdur Rahman in 1895, thus transforming Afghan Kafiristan, "the land of the unclean," into Nuristan, "the land of the pure." In Chitral, in Pakistan, the Kafirs are not exposed to religious or racial persecution or forcible conversion, but as a minute minority they are being increasingly assimilated to their Islamic environment. An "anthropological paradise," as the scientists call it, is disappearing.

The gods of the Kafirs are manifold, constituting something like a Greek pantheon. There are a few principal deities, universally recognized, but in addition, each valley, sometimes each village, has its own local gods.

62

The chief god, Imra—called Khodai by the priest in the Brumburet Valley—has no form and is omnipresent. He created human beings (from a butter sack) and gave them souls. He also created dogs to wake mankind from sleep. Some believe that he has withdrawn to heaven, whence he observes his creation "through a sliding window in his beard," but others hold that he still tarries among men, disguised as a beggar. Imra is no Creator and Almighty God in the Christian sense, but rather a helper of humanity. When he invented the water mill he built one of wheaten dough and drove it with goat's milk, and the assistance of the goddess Lunang was needed before a more practical model of stone and wood was produced. He owes his position of leader to shrewdness with an admixture of impudence. Once, for instance, all the gods were assembled on a hilltop, where stood a golden bed. "It belongs to all of us together," they said. "No, to me only," said Imra, seating himself on it. The other gods were dumbfounded.

In former days, when the Kafirs were combative, great importance attached to Gish, the god of war. Speaking through the mouths of priests in a state of trance, he would choose an opponent, generally weaker, and order a campaign against him. He filled his leisure hours by playing polo with the skulls of fallen warriors. He came into being through a creative word uttered by Indra, the Hindu war god of the time of the Vedas, or alternatively he was born through the navel of a woman after a pregnancy of eighteen months.

The other gods, such as Balumain, Mahadeo, or Kushumai, resemble the ministers and secretaries of state of a modern government in that each has his own department such as weather, harvest, herds, or health. In case of need, application for advice or assistance is made to the competent god, the forwarding of petitions to the heavenly authorities being undertaken by the priests.

The priestly office is not hereditary, being filled by those who receive a call from "a distant voice," the man called being unable to tell whether it comes from a god or the fairies. Such a call usually comes to a man in middle age, leaving him in a confused mental state for several months. At the end of that period he is washed in the blood of a sacrificed goat, whereupon his mind suddenly becomes clear and rational. He has no need of instruction concerning the remote divine world with which he now becomes a mediator, for this heaven is revealed to him in a flash. Since nowadays the Kafir gods are neither cruel nor demanding, the priests do not play a dominant role in everyday life; they keep their herds and fields, their families and their poor clothing, and are required to establish communication with the gods only on special occasions. These last are generally celebrations, which, however, are not bound to either a particular place or a particular ritual, and the communication is established by inhaling the smoke of burning juniper twigs, inducing a trance in which the priest can hear the wishes, counsels, or commands of the gods. Like the shamans of Siberia, they possess great mediumistic powers, being able in the state of trance not only to cure illness and foretell the future, but also to "find" lost articles. The state of prophetic exaltation often used to be induced by dancing, flute playing or drum beating, but nowadays juniper smoke is mostly used.

Together with an Austrian friend I witnessed such a consultation with the gods in the Brumburet Valley on the occasion of the festival of Chilimjust, which is celebrated in May. It might be called the "festival of the high pastures," for it was the season at which the herds are driven up into the mountains. A return of winter weather with snowfalls was feared—reason enough to consult the gods. The beginning was a little monotonous. Men and women formed groups, singing and dancing—always the same melancholy tunes and the same steps. In this way the morning passed, and only then did the consultation of the priests begin. At this stage the women were excluded, and we men went a few hundred yards uphill to a sacred place in the shadow of a mighty nut tree. A fire was lighted, and the two priests, peasants with whom we had made friends but whom we had not yet seen in the execution of their office, inhaled the biting juniper smoke in deep breaths. They fell into their trance quickly—so quickly that the suspicion of playacting, unfounded though it certainly was, did occur to us. In any case they acted the part magnificently, with empty faces which were nevertheless expressive of listening to the inner world.

The faithful might now put their questions to the gods. Khodai himself is too great to be importuned with trifles, but his two "ministers," Balumain and Mahadeo, answered willingly. The questions were of a practical nature: "Will my cow recover?" "Should I drive my goats into the Birir Valley?" "Will it snow again on the mountain pastures?" "Will there be a good harvest?" The gods gave suitably matter-of-fact answers, adding that the sacrifice of a goat would be acceptable, but since the meat is shared among all the inhabitants of the village, neither priests nor gods can be accused of self-seeking.

We ourselves asked how long we would stay in Kafiristan and whether we should reach our homeland safely, and the god correctly prophesied both the length of our stay, which at that time had not been decided, and our safe return.

Budok, the priest to whom we were particularly attached, is very highly thought of, for all that he goes around in rags. In 1948 the gods informed him that a typhoid epidemic was due to break out in Rumbur, so he informed the inhabitants, urging them to make an appropriate sacrifice. But his warning was ignored, and it was only after six people had died that Budok was called in to make peace with the gods and so put a stop to the ravages of the disease.

The Kafirs live in a world ruled by supernatural powers, and they have to be very careful not to violate any of their laws or taboos. There are three worlds or spheres. One is impure (hell), one human (this world), and the third pure (heaven).

Chickens are regarded as unclean, and so is a journey beyond the frontiers of Kafiristan. In former times a ceremonial purification was carried out when a Kafir returned from Chitral.

Women are not "clean" enough to milk the highly prized cows and goats; strictly speaking, they may not even set foot in a barn. In consequence they labor in the fields, while the men, once their milking is done, have ample leisure.

Menstruating and pregnant women are seriously unclean. Babies are not born at home, but in a special birthhouse standing apart, in which no man ever sets foot. If birth occurs in winter, the midwives must perform their task naked. The husband may not resume intercourse with his wife until four months after a birth.

Cemeteries likewise are unclean. The heavy wooden coffins are not buried but lie on the surface, exposed to wind and weather. Between the coffins stand human figures carved in wood; they represent not gods but respected citizens who once bequeathed the population a funeral feast. The

64

41 Glacier-covered pass in Chitral, used by the local people in summer

carvings also frequently represent the heads of horses or a rider on a two-headed horse. The meaning of these horses is not clear; could they be renderings of the formless god Mahadeo? A two-headed horse is shown on the coins of King Kanishka of the Kushan kingdom; might the traditions of the Kafirs reach so far back?

Once, having time on my hands, I wandered at leisure through the three valleys, attuning myself to their peaceful, rather melancholy workaday life, and in this way I learned to understand the superstitions of the Kafirs.

In former times, life was far pleasanter, for gods, spirits, and men lived peacefully together, although, it is true, there were no animals. The spirits helped with the work, but when the human beings interfered with them, whether by accident or design, they withdrew.

The female spirits, who are called Balo, sometimes put on the form of women and return to earth, where they may marry. The husband of a Balo enjoys many advantages, for not only does his wife work hard in the fields, but she also retains her connection with the male spirits, or Yush, and these know all the best places for game, so the husband must inevitably become a successful hunter.

Matrimonial triangles in which no spirits are involved must be purged by blood, but not, as in neighboring Chitral, the blood of the lover and probably of the faithless wife as well, but that of a goat, provided by the disturber of the matrimonial harmony and eaten in company by those concerned. An exacting husband may also claim damages up to six cows, and it is rumored that mercenary-minded couples have been known to acquire considerable herds in this way.

I remember my last evening in Kafiristan. To avoid returning to Chitral too soon, I had to fill in a day in the wretched village of Guru. The landscape here is dominated by nut trees—it must be a delight to travel here in the nut season—and a bedstead for me had been placed under one of them. A few hungry dogs and innumerable hungry mosquitoes circled round, and my interpreter, Samad, and I drowsed away the time.

An old man, dignified despite his rags, came and talked insistently. He stammered, and Samad took no pains with his story, so I understood only its broad outlines; but it was peculiar, and it made me sad to think that in a generation or two the Kafirs will be no more than a memory.

The life of a herdsman on the high pastures, the old man said, is very lonely, but also very wholesome. He is generally a young man, and he is alone with his beasts and close to heaven; he lives on milk, cheese, chapati bread, and an occasional piece of meat. At the end of the long summer he is bursting with health and animal spirits, and when he returns to the valley, he is allowed to spend the first night with the woman of his choice, even though she be married—at least that is how it was in the old days. The child of such a union is held in great honor, for the spirit of the high pastures lives in it.

A very pretty story, and Samad asked if it was true. Of course it was, the old man sniggered, for he had been a herdsman himself, and here, he said, fumbling from his rags a silver ring set with a coral, was his memento of such a night.

The coral gleamed dully, and Samad said that all that must have happened many, many years ago. The old man drew pensively on a cigarette I had given him and nodded.

Being separated from Afghanistan by difficult passes and a political frontier, the Kafirs come into contact only with their other neighbors, the Chitralis. Sir George Robertson, who made war on the latter at the turn of the century, gives an unflattering account of them: "There are few more treacherous people in the world than the Chitralis, who have a particular talent for cold-blooded murder." Either Sir George exaggerated or the Chitralis have changed, for the peace-loving Kafirs suffer no oppression from them. The Mulk family, the rulers of Chitral, who trace their descent back to Timur Leng (Tamerlare), have preserved a certain degree of independence within Pakistan, and they maintain law and order in their territory. Perhaps this was not so in earlier times. Visitors to their castle in Chitral are informed, before each portrait of an ancestor, whom he murdered and who murdered him, and a questioning glance elicits a sly smile and the reply "What do you expect? Natural selection: The most capable becomes the ruler."

The Hunzas are better known than either the Kafirs or the Chitralis. This small people lives north of Gilgit in a lovely valley of the Karakorum—and principally on apricots, which are called the gold of the Hunzas. They cultivate twenty different varieties which blossom and ripen in succession, thus leaving more time for picking. Fresh and dried apricots, together with chapati bread, form the diet of the Hunzas, and investigators once reported that they were the healthiest people in the world, entirely free of disease. Good times followed for manufacturers of nature food and growers of apricots—until closer investigation revealed that the Hunzas are in no way healthier than we are, for the diseases of civilization have not yet reached them.

Valle Bellissima

The opening up of the Himalayas, and the climbing of the 26,000 foot peaks, which has proceeded with such rapidity in recent years, was made possible by a socialist revolution which helped a king who is an incarnation of the god Vishnu to return to power. Such a paradoxical situation could certainly arise only in Nepal, and it is a fact that an almost bloodless rebellion, supported by India, broke the rule of the Rana family, who had held the kings in subjection for a century and had closed the country completely to all foreigners. Since eight of the 26,000-footers lie in Nepal, and Communist Tibet had closed the way to the frontier mountains, the "opening" of Nepal came just in time to enable the Englishman John Hunt, the New Zealander Edmund P. Hillary, and party to lay the conquest of the highest mountain in the world at their queen's feet on the day of her coronation.

The rich valleys of Nepal favor agriculture and the formation of comparatively large settlements, and for this reason the history of the country is more strongly determined by geographical conditions than is that of others in the Himalayas. Mongoloid tribes came down over the passes from the north, while Aryan groups forced their way upward from the south. Both found a climatic frontier, the former being unwilling to penetrate farther to the hot south, the latter not wishing to go on into the northern cold. Thus the ethnological map of Nepal corresponds almost exactly to the isothermic

67

42 Ancestral castle of the princes of Hunza in Baltit

43 Nameless peak (23,000 feet) and glacier stream in the Muztagh-Karakorum

44 The Shayok Valley in the eastern Karakorum. Meandering rivulets are in the riverbed before the monsoon

45 Abandoned caves, once inhabited, in the northern-most part of Nepal, near the Tibetan frontier

46 Terraced fields and peach trees in the eastern Kara-korum, about 9,000 feet

47 Hills in central Nepal covered by hundreds of ter-races

48 Village well in Tibet

49 The *chautarrah*, a platform to facilitate taking off loads carried on the back, is frequently found on the footways in Nepal

50 and 51 Nepalese children

52 Sherpa festivity in Khumjung, Mount Everest area

53 Lamas of Tengpoche, Mount Everest area

54 and 55 Nepalese types

56 "Horses' heads" connected with the Kafir religion

57 "Modern" paintings offer protection against spirits in Bangthari, Nepal

58 and 59 Sherpa children

60 A lama with the "scalp of the yeti"

61 to 64 Specimens of the "dok-pa," protectors against all kinds of evil in western Nepal

65 Clay tiger as temple guardian

66 Prayer flags in a Himalayan wind. In the background is Mount Kangtega (22,300 feet). Northern Nepal

67 Clear as a mirror: a glacier lake in the Himalayas

one. The frontier between the Hinduism of the south and the Lamaism of the north likewise follows lines of relief and temperature, a mixed region lying between in which—particularly in and around Katmandu—the two religions intermingle in felicitous harmony in a wide variety of artistic forms. If India had been spared the conquests by Islam and the British, its life and culture would be reminiscent of Nepal, where the various immigrants seldom came into conflict since they were not disputing the same living space. Nevertheless, Nepal's history was anything but peaceful; the bellicose temperament of the Gurkhas saw to that.

When the Buddha was born in the small town of Rummindei, now in Nepalese territory, the Kirantis, the predecessors of the Newaris, ruled the Nepal Valley. The Newar rulers found more joy in philosophy and religion than in waging war, and in their time the Valley of Nepal was transformed into a treasure-house of fine architectural and artistic works in such numbers as are rarely found in such a small area. The "Valley of Nepal" is the name given to the fruitful plain surrounding the three royal cities of Katmandu, Patan, and Bhadgaon, the center from which outlying districts were conquered. Today the native on his way to Katmandu still says he is going "to Nepal," and the Gurkha, asked what his country is, replies, not "Nepal," but "Pahar—the hills."

The physical rule of the Newaris, did not extend beyond the frontiers of the valley, but their art still dominates extensive areas of Asia. The Nepalese architect Aruibo was brought by Kublai Khan to Peking, where he worked many years, and it is fairly certain that the type of the many-storied pagoda came from Katmandu to Peking, and not the other way.

During the last centuries before the Gurkha rule the dynasty of the Malla came to power. The name means literally boxer or conqueror, but the Malla rulers failed to live up to it, carrying on the traditional patronage of the fine arts. This patronage was responsible for the greater part of the architectural, sculptural, and other monuments which still delight every visitor to Nepal. Although

46

48

49

50

51

52

53

54

55

56

57

58

59

61, 62

63, 64

themselves strict Hindus, they opened their kingdom, which was later to become "the most strictly closed country in the world," to Christian missionaries. At the beginning of the eighteenth century the Capuchins established a hospice—a branch of their settlement in Lhasa—in Katmandu, and when Father Horatius della Penna, falling victim to the machinations of jealous Brahmins, was condemned to slave labor, he made such an impression on the king with the catechism he had compiled in the Newar language that permission to preach was restored to him.

Another Capuchin told of a *valle bellissima* which at first glance seemed to be made of gold, so numerous were its pagodas and gilded palaces. "The air is mild and wholesome; there is abundance of every kind of foodstuff; nearly every variety of fruit which we know in Europe grows here."

The fathers who were so enthusiastic over their new province must have lowered their eyes bashfully before the images of so many divinities who take such evident pleasure in erotic diversions. In serious-minded India the symbolic aspect of such representations is emphasized, but in Nepal a more graceful explanation has been devised: These figures, which have become a popular lure for tourists, are simply lightning conductors. For the lightning, being as everybody knows a virgin, at the sight of such naturalistic representations retires blushing to the heavens, leaving the earth unharmed.

The Hindu refugees from India who once, under pressure from the Moslems, sought safety and a new home in the mountains of Nepal belonged for the most part to the two highest castes, the priests and the warriors. The members of lower castes had less to fear from the Moslems, and in any case less to lose; perhaps they also lacked the strength and the resources for the flight to a distant country. In this way it came about that some settlements in Nepal were principally inhabited by Brahmins and Kshatriyas, who in India formed only the upper 10,000 among the population.

Among the refugees from Chitor, in Rajputana, the military qualities must have greatly outweighed the priestly tendencies, for within a few generations they had overthrown the Newar kings and imposed the Gurkha rule on the whole of Nepal. The name is taken from the little mountain town where they first settled. In 1766 their king Prithwi Narayan eliminated all local rivals and founded a self-contained country and a dynasty which survives to this day, despite a history of bloody intrigues and betrayals reminiscent of Shakespeare's historical plays. The present King Mahendra Bir Bikram Shah Deva is a direct descendant of Prithwi Narayan.

About the middle of the nineteenth century a new power arose out of the chaos produced by the intrigues of weak kings, power-hungry widows, and heirs not yet of age. The young nobleman Jang Bahadur usurped the supreme authority, making the office of Prime Minister hereditary, so that henceforth his family, the Rana, like the shoguns in Japan or the Merovingian mayors of the palace, ruled the land dictatorially. The kings—in this case at the same time gods—were held prisoners in a golden cage. The "Ranachy" had begun.

Jang Bahadur's was a personality compounded of political vision, great personal courage, Oriental cruelty, and—circumstances permitting—surprising magnanimity. The stories about him are legion.

Thus, for instance, he proposed to his youthful heir, who grudged him both his influence and his life, that he, Jang, should throw himself into a deep well. The suggestion was graciously accepted, and before a throng of spectators Jang made the deadly leap. His body was heard to strike the water far below. In the night his friends, seeking the corpse, found him clinging to the stonework of the well shaft.

When he was only thirty-two, he decided that his power was well enough consolidated for him to make a state visit to England. He was the first Hindu ruler to cross the "black water" to the land of the unclean, and he risked the loss of his caste. On his return, despite subjecting himself to lengthy purifications in Benares, he did in fact have difficulties with the Brahmins.

In London the exotic young potentate was the event of the season; Queen Victoria herself was delighted with him. He moved through the drawing rooms with complete naturalness and rose to every occasion with charm and diplomatic finesse. In face of the many-sided Rana personality the ruthlessness with which he had seized power was forgotten.

Although he had privately expressed the opinion that he found operatic performances crazy and tedious, he took a box for the duration of his visit. On one occasion he sat beside the queen, who noticed that he applauded enthusiastically when the curtain fell.

"But you didn't understand what was being sung?" she said in surprise.

"No, ma'am," replied Jang. "No more than I understand what the nightingales are saying."

In the twenty years of life that remained to him, he made the frontiers secure and established a firmly knit state. When he died, he was not only feared and hated, but also admired and loved. Although he had criticized the Hindu custom of suttee his three maharanis ascended the funeral pyre. Before going to her voluntary death, the senior wife addressed the assembled mourners:

"Gentlemen, you all know what love the maharaja bore you and with what devotion he dedicated himself to the welfare of his country. If in the execution of his duty he ever wronged any one of you in word or deed I beg you in his name to forgive him and to join me in praying for the eternal rest of his soul." She thereupon entered the flames.

I have described Jang Bahadur thus fully because Nepal still bears the imprint of his personality. The Ranas closed the country against all external influence and all change. Their word alone was the law of the land, and they accumulated incredible wealth. After their deposition a single one of their golden crowns was sold to the King of Saudi Arabia for something like $2,500,000. They modeled their residences on Versailles and Buckingham palaces. The government palace Singh-Durbar is said to contain 1,200 rooms; nobody knows the exact number, but the leaders of expeditions will remember their visits there as an exhausting preparation for pathfinding in the Himalayas.

Although the Ranas, for strategic reasons, allowed no roads to be built to India, they did not want to forgo the use of the new automobiles, so a few miles of asphalt were laid in Katmandu, and the automobiles were carried up over the foothills of the Himalayas by coolies in the course of a three-month portage.

The Ranas knew how to live. When the Nepalese Prime Minister-Maharaja visited India in 1880, his retinue consisted of 15 maharanis, 40 generals, colonels and other officers, 300 miscellaneous staff, 50 musicians and 50 women servants. Even the British, who did indeed themselves set store by magnificence and display in India, were impressed.

86

The Ranas also knew how to entertain—when the guest was worth the trouble. When King George V visited South Nepal on a hunting expedition, the maharaja provided 600 elephants and 10,000 Gurkha soldiers, as well as electric lights and hot and cold running water in the wilds.

It would not have been possible for the Ranas to maintain their autocratic regime for so long without the goodwill of Britain, but the Mother of Parliaments had no objection to dictatorships on the confines of her empire, provided that they formed reliable buffer states. And Nepal was more than that—it was a loyal ally which voluntarily took the British side in the Indian Mutiny of 1857 and in both world wars.

Independent India with its democratic ideas inevitably meant the end of the Ranas. Many Nepalese, among them even Rana supporters dissatisfied with the disposition of power, were living in exile in India. Under Nehru they found the moral and material support that had been denied them by the British. The revolt against the Ranas began in November, 1950, in circumstances partly obscure, partly romantic. King Tribhuvan took advantage of a hunting expedition to seek refuge within the walls of the Indian Embassy in Katmandu, and despite the protest of Mohan Shamsher, the last Rana ruler, he was flown to India. The German sick nurse Erika Leuchttag, who had come to Katmandu to tend the ailing maharani, played an exciting role as go-between for the king and Nehru, and her book *Erika und der König (Erika and the King)* is as thrilling to read as a romantically tinted spy best seller. Shamsher abdicated, the Nepalese Congress Party took over the government, and the king returned to his throne as a monarch; the frontiers were opened, and the period of the great expeditions began. The visitors, filled with admiration and astonishment, realized that the seventeenth-century Capuchin father had not exaggerated, for the "most beautiful valley" in the world, with golden pagodas and silver snow-mountains shining in the sun, did in fact lie before them.

This short retrospect of Nepalese history, with its all-powerful maharajas, might lead one to expect to find a timid, down-trodden, and mistrustful populace, but the truth is the exact opposite. In 1953 I traveled through the country for several months, being in some districts the first white man the people had ever seen. The government in Katmandu had kindly given me a letter of recommendation, instructing the mukias, or headmen, of the villages to sell me milk, firewood, and food at the normal prices.

In one tiny village we found the mukia busy repairing his felt shoes, and he continued morosely with his work, paying no heed to the government instructions.

"At least stand up when you speak to a white sahib," my Sherpas demanded.

"How could I ever get anything finished if I was always doing that?" he demanded.

"How many sahibs have you seen in your life?" the Sherpas asked.

"This is the first" said the mukia, and went on sewing.

The Rana dictatorship seems to have had no ill effects on this refreshing independence of spirit among the villagers or on their hospitality, which would be overwhelming if it were not so much a part of everyday life that one takes it for granted. With an expedition or on roads where the inhabitants have been "spoiled" by tourists, one does not notice this quality so much, but alone or with no more than two or three companions, one never need worry, if the district is inhabited at all, about a roof over one's head. One can—and this is hardly an exaggeration—enter a house without greeting or explanation and simply spend the night there. Generally the arrival is accompanied by small talk and an exchange of presents, the host giving eggs or milk, the guest money or tobacco—but silence would not be resented. True, the equipment of the houses is generally confined to an earth floor, but during a wet night the roof is no small consideration. Once in a rain storm that overtook me on the much-frequented trade route between Langtrang Himal and Katmandu, I found shelter in one such hospitable house. It was full to bursting point with other shelter seekers, but more and more soaked wayfarers continued to squeeze themselves in. As an early arrival I felt that I had almost the rights of a tenant, and I was inclined to object to this excessive hospitality, bound up as it was with crowding, coughing, spitting and other forms of humidity. When I spoke to my host about it, he declared with satisfaction that he need never, rain or shine, complain of an empty house. The Nepalese say, "Where there is a heart, there is always room," and their hearts must be very large, since they are able to pack so many people into them.

This hospitality not only has sentimental value as an expression of feeling, but is also of great practical significance, for the Nepalese are a people of wayfarers. Although the majority of small settlements are self-supporting, long files of heavily laden people are always to be met with on the footpaths. The principal reason for this itinerancy is salt, which is not found in Nepal. Since there is no organized system of retail trade, each household must make its own arrangements to obtain salt, and since the frontier with Tibet, formerly an important supplier, has been closed for political reasons, it must be brought from India. During the winter months some of the members of each peasant family pack a little agricultural produce into carrying baskets and set out on a march lasting several weeks in order to trade it for salt at a market in India. It sounds like a burdensome trudge, but for the peasants it is a pleasant excursion on which they thoroughly enjoy themselves. Dr. Toni Hagen, who spent several years traveling in Nepal, estimates that every year some 2,000,000 people, or one-quarter of the total population, are on the march in this way for from four to eight weeks. The universal hospitality—exemplified by the *chautarrahs*, the stone walls built mostly in the shade of a tree or near a spring, inviting the traveler to deposit his load on them, or the taverns at which he can drink a few mouthfuls of chang as he passes—helps transform the arduous salt pilgrimage into a cheerful picnic.

The World's Best Soldiers

In a remote valley in northeastern Nepal a peasant greeted me with effusive cordiality and in surprisingly good English. From his military bearing and the way he addressed me as "Captain Sahib," he was obviously a Gurkha, a member of the warrior tribe who, according to people who should know, make the world's best soldiers. In both world wars they served with the British forces in Asia, Africa, and Europe: at Gallipoli and on the Suez Canal, in Cyprus; and at El Alamein, Tobruk,

68 A sacred cow in Katmandu

and Monte Cassino. Their courage and discipline are dreaded and admired, as the case may be, by friend and foe alike.

After recovering from his disappointment that I was not a captain sahib, and on hearing that I came from Germany—I could hardly expect him ever to have heard of Austria—his delight knew no bounds. He had met many Germans, he said. He had fought against them in North Africa and (at this point he visibly swelled with sporting pride) had managed to kill one or two, not only at long range with his rifle but also with his kukri (here his fingers played lovingly over the Nepalese knife stuck in his belt). Because the conversation was becoming unpleasantly akin to "shop," I asked him about the harvest prospects. There had hardly been any monsoon at all that summer, and the peasants were grumbling about the drought. My Gurkha friend explained that he personally was all right, for his annual pension of about $50 a year, about five times as much as the average peasant's income, meant that he and his family would be able to make ends meet. On active service he earned more than $250 a year—i.e. twenty-five times as much as the average peasant had to live on, and since he neither drank nor gambled, he remitted it all to his family in Nepal. I figured that Gurkha soldiers must constitute an important item in the Nepal budget if their military prowess brings in a total of about $4,800,000 a year.

The Gurkhas are descended from Rajputan warriors who many years ago were forced by Moslem pressure to take to the mountains in the northern part of the country, where after protracted fighting they vanquished the ruling Malla Dynasty and eventually founded what is now Nepal. They are named after the ancient town of Gurkha from which King Prithwi Narayan set out to make war on and subdue the local dynastic princes. Most of the Nepalese soldiers who achieved fame as Gurkhas were ethnologically not really Gurkhas at all but were members of other warlike tribes such as the Gurung, Magar, Rai, Tamang, and Limbu.

After Prithwi Narayan had consolidated his hold over his territory, Nepal became involved in hostilities with Britain and was defeated in two hard-fought campaigns. But the pride and courage of the Gurkhas so impressed the British that the peace terms were distinctly lenient, and the opponents of yesterday became the allies of today who were either treated as equals or kept at a respectful distance. During the Indian Mutiny in 1857 the ruler of Nepal, Jang Bahadur, came to the help of the British, who showed their gratitude by giving him back some of the territory he had been obliged to cede. But this did not prevent him from granting the rebel leaders asylum, a characteristic gesture that was intended to demonstrate the independence and sovereignty of his country. The British resident in Katmandu enjoyed precious little freedom of movement, and when the British viceroy, Lord Curzon, expressed the wish to visit Nepal, he was given to understand that the moment he retired from public life he would be more than welcome, but that as viceroy he would not be admitted.

The Gurkhas' proud spirit and their bulldog tenacity in adversity may well have awakened kindred feelings in the British; anyway, with their rulers' consent the Gurkhas became some of the British Empire's doughtiest warriors. Fifty thousand of them fought in the First World War, and 250,000 in the second (though the exact figures vary from one authority to another). Today 8,000 of them are still serving in the British army, and 12,000 in the Indian.

Along with the Swiss Guards at the Vatican and the white soldiers who fought in the Congo, the Gurkhas are the last of the mercenaries. There may well be disapproval on ethical grounds of their readiness to fight anyone anywhere, but they are real "troopers" who enjoy fighting for its own sake. When Singapore surrendered to the Japanese, the Gurkhas were the last to cease fire. In Burma they fought against imperialism, in Malaya they helped put down the Communist insurrection, and today they are posted on the bridge at Lowu, the frontier between Hong Kong and China. They may not be particularly interested in how or why a war started, but once they are in it, they kill and are killed in astonishingly cold blood.

Most Gurkhas are Hindus, and their society is based on caste. When they went to war against Tibet in the nineteenth century, they almost starved for lack of eatable food, because yak meat is tabu, yaks being akin to cows, which are sacred. The Gurkhas, who usually win their campaigns, almost came to grief this time, and they were saved only by the resourceful Brahmins, who eventually pronounced the yak to be a species of overgrown deer.

One would have thought that after having been on the winning side in so many European campaigns—and how magnificent their bearing was at the victory parade in London—the Gurkhas would have sown the seeds of discontent in the remote valleys of their native land by introducing alien ideas and practices. Far from it. Take my new friend, for instance, who was all cordiality and genuine goodwill. The fact that he had killed human beings who spoke the same language as I do was not allowed to come between us in any way. We were brothers and slept under his hospitable roof. I did not dare ask him why his village seemed never to have heard of the wheel, although he must have traveled hundreds of miles in jeeps, or why his pastures were so desolate, although his eyes must have feasted on the corn of Italy and the grapes of France. He had not brought any subversive ideas home with him; only a few memories, his savings, and his pension. A typical mercenary's homecoming, in fact.

The Great Mountain Guides

The Sherpas need no introduction. For such a small community they have a unique place in the world's respect and affection. But it would be well to correct at the outset the popular misconception that *sherpa* means guide or mountain porter. In point of fact the word is a blend of *shar*, meaning east, and *pa*, meaning person or people—*i.e.* "east people." In Nepal, to the south of Mount Everest, they are concentrated mainly in the Khumbu and Solu areas. As their name implies, they arrived a century or two ago from the east, from Khan, in eastern Tibet. What with the barrenness of their new home and their inborn love of exploration some of them found their way to Darjeeling, where they founded a Sherpa colony. Early in the 1920's they began to be taken on as porters by British Himalayan expeditions and soon proved themselves first-class climbers. But they were sought after and respected not so much for their physical attributes as for their sterling human qualities, which made them wonderful companions.

In the checkered history of Himalayan exploration there have been many instances of Sherpas giving their lives for the white sahib or of sharing a dying comrade's fate rather than abandon him. I know of no instance of a Sherpa ever being open to a charge of cowardice or shirking, although I am not entirely objective. I have spent many weeks of my life with them, which is bound to make one prejudiced. But the onetime Himalaya Club at Darjeeling, which used to keep an accurate register of Sherpa porters, can certainly not be accused of prejudice or favoritism. Every Sherpa was given a number to prevent any mix-up over his name, since all Sherpa names sound rather alike. Sherpas are very often named after the day of the week they were born on: Nima–Sunday, Dawa–Monday, Pasang–Friday, Pemba–Saturday. The registry contained details of the expeditions a Sherpa had been on and of his efficiency and individual characteristics. An entry regarding performance which frequently puzzled the uninitiated was: "Above chang line excellent." Chang is a sort of beer that the Sherpas brew from barley or some similar grain and drink in vast quantities. Many of them, even the most renowned mountaineers, tend to lose sight of their purpose and discipline when passing through their native villages. Any abstemious leader of an expedition will heave a sigh of relief once he has got his Sherpas safely through the "beer line."

Personally I do not grudge the Sherpas their fondness for alcohol. When I was climbing Cho Oyu, which is well over 26,000 feet high, my hands got severely frostbitten, and it looked as if I should lose a finger or two. When I presented myself at the clinic in Vienna, the doctor looked first at the photographs of my hands taken in the Himalayas and then at the hands themselves. "You should by rights have lost one or two fingers," he said reproachfully, "but I don't think we shall have to operate. Did you use any particular preparation?" I told him I had had the usual Padutin and Ronicol injections, plus ointment and massage. He was amazed, had never seen anything like it in all his long experience of frostbite on the Russian front. He asked whether I had kept to any particular diet or regime. "Yes," I admitted, "on the way down we were either tipsy or completely sozzled for two whole weeks." "Well, that's what saved your hands. As you know, alcohol dilates the blood vessels and stimulates the circulation." Of course the healing properties of alcohol was the last thing we thought of as we submitted to the feasting and hospitality of the Khumbu and Solu Sherpa villages on the way down from Cho Oyu. I must admit that the ceremonies were not so much in honor of us three Austrians as of Pasang Dawa Lama, our *sirdar* (leader) and a countryman of our hosts. But since we had all been on the same expedition and the chang had been paid for out of the expedition's funds, we were included in the celebrations and had to comport ourselves according to the laws of hospitality. These were often rigid and inexorable. The valley was so narrow that it was impossible to go around a village, and in any case our approach had already been announced by gongs or trumpets. Three or four women would be standing in a row at the entrance to the village holding out brass platters of chang, with little lumps of yak butter on the side. We were supposed to drink an individual toast with everyone present, draining each platter three times, but more often than not we failed to complete the course, because we were either tired after an allnight dance we had had to attend or we were saving ourselves for similar festivities in the near future.

But it is not only on festive occasions that Sherpas display such a positive attitude to life. Even in the tightest corner they never lose their optimism, and when things are really desperate, they are still perfectly calm and phlegmatic. Once when a storm looked as if it were about to blow away our solitary tent from the crest of Gurla Mandhata in Tibet, my Sherpa Kitar said it was "the gods," and during a perishingly cold night's bivouac Pasang admitted that "it wasn't as warm as it is in the kitchen." It certainly wasn't. Only once did Pasang lose his nerve. When a storm on Cho Oyu destroyed our tents and we were sure we should never get down alive, he burst into tears and exclaimed, "Die!" Even that was quite an achievement, because at the time I personally was unable to raise either a voice or a tear.

The Sherpas occupied a unique position among Himalayan peoples long before the arrival of European expeditions and the opening up of new careers as mountaineers. This was due to their quick intelligence, as well as to the geographical situation of their native land. A trade route to Tibet via Nangpa La (18,863 feet) runs right through their territory, and the village of Namche Bazar (a name that crops up in the reports of any number of expeditions) became an important trading center. Traders from Tibet brought wool and, even more important, salt, a vital commodity not found in Nepal, while exports northward included sugar, rice, paper, and sundry primitive industrial products. The Sherpas exploited their position and in time managed to get a monopoly. Because they are also excellent cattle breeders and the pastures on the southern slopes of the Himalayas are greener than in arid Tibet, they can export yaks and butter. Many Sherpas have traveled far and wide looking for trade and are equally at home in Lhasa or Calcutta. Curiously enough, they are regarded as shrewd businessmen, although their reputation for honesty is above suspicion.

Often enough, pure chance seems to have had a hand in their fortunes. Take the import of potatoes, for instance. Nobody knows for certain when and by whom they were introduced to the Sherpa country, although a fifty-year-old Sherpa claimed that as a child he had known an old man who had planted the first potatoes. Today, in any settlement more than 10,000 feet above sea level, potatoes, buckwheat, turnips, and a species of spinach are the staple foods.

Human habitation is found at what by European standards are astonishing heights. Any sizable village has its satellite settlements that are occupied or abandoned according to the time of year. These gunsa are at a lower altitude than the parent village and are particularly popular during the very cold winter months. They also provide arable land. In the summer the flocks are driven up to high pastures called phu, which can sometimes be utilized for growing hay and potatoes. The highest settlements of all, the desolate resa, are usually on stony soil and are used only by shepherds for an occasional night or two.

Details of Sherpa settlements in Khumbu show that the highest permanent settlement is at Panghoche (13,173 feet), the highest pasture is at Lobuche (16,270 feet), the highest grazing is at 17,650 feet, barley and potatoes are found at up to 14,520 feet, and the snowline is at 17,500 feet.

The Sherpa villages are not unlike communities in the Alps. All houses are built on the same plan, with two stories, and are kept at a respectful distance from one another by little fields. The ground floor serves as a fuel and wood store and in the winter as a stable. A steep flight of stairs leads up to the top floor, the pattern of which is invariably the same: an open fireplace opposite the stairs and, along the wall, a long seat with a special place next to the fire for the master of the house.

Household articles, supplies, clothes, and other chattels are stored along the walls or hung from the ceiling. There is usually a bed in a small niche, but the household often sleeps on skins or rugs spread out in front of the fire. Particularly pious and well-to-do families curtain off part of the room as a sort of sanctum, with a statue of the Buddha decked with religious pictures and devotional objects. The sanctum is also a useful place to dump a sack or two of potatoes or a barrel of chang (the Sherpas are adept at combining religious observance with creature comforts). In a popular household the entire space around the fire will be taken up by a gathering of old friends; if, on the other hand, peace and quiet are what is required, the sanctum affords a sanctuary of absolute privacy from which the social gathering not more than a yard or two away can be rejoined at will. For sufferers from severe frostbite the sanctum is an ideal blend of tavern and a private room in a hospital, as I found out for myself at Namche Bazar.

As regards religion, race, and culture, the Sherpas are closely akin to their northern neighbors, the Tibetans. In the event of Chinese rule in Tibet abolishing the old customs, especially the traditional way of life in the monasteries, the Sherpa country, along with Ladakh, Sikkim, and Bhutan, will be the last repository of this ancient civilization. Admittedly the Dalai Lama sought sanctuary in the Indian Himalaya, not in Nepal, but the abbot of the monastery at Rongphur (celebrated for its contribution to Mount Everest expeditions) is now living in Nepal.

The Sherpas' way of life is by no means tabu-ridden. Instead of castes there are from eighteen to twenty-one clans, and to prevent inbreeding, intermarriage is not allowed. As well as the "genuine" Sherpas, there are the Khambas. Although their language and way of life differ little from those of the Sherpas, they are regarded as inferior. They are usually taken on as seasonal workers with nothing to their name but "a stick and a basket," as the Sherpa capitalists put it. But they too can work their way up to a fair measure of prosperity and esteem. The celebrated "Sherpa" Tensing, for instance, is a Khamba; so is the Abbot of Tengboche. Like the Sherpas, the Khambas have abjured the caste system except that smiths and slaughterers are rather looked down on.

The "democratic" nature of the Sherpas' social structure is matched by the extraordinary freedom of their family and marital code. Premarital intercourse is not a sin, and illegitimate children are seldom something to be ashamed of. A betrothal is an interminable proceeding with an array of suitors, gallons of chang, and strict ceremonial ritual. Adultery rarely leads to a *crime passionnel;* it is usually enough for the guilty party to pay a fine as a token of contrition. If he is a friend of the family or even an abbot, the husband is expected to turn a blind eye. A woman can have two or more husbands, and this polyandry has the advantage that the man does not have to share all his worldly goods and that during the long business expeditions there is always one husband to look after the home and the animals. Since all of the wife's children have equal rights, there is no need for frantic speculation on which of the husbands is the father. But once a monogamous marriage has been entered into, it is not lawful for the woman to take a second husband. Divorce is in certain circumstances a relatively straightforward business, and it speaks for the Sherpas' commonsense attitude in these matters that both parties get off as lightly as possible.

Although the children have to start working in the fields at an early age and even act as beasts of burden, the grown-ups almost smother them with loving care. I have never known (often to my regret) a Sherpa child get the walloping he deserved, and once they have got over their first shyness, Sherpa children can be as charmingly irritating as little monkeys. Although they grow up into such superb mountaineers, it is a long time before they are taught to walk, sometimes not until they are four years old. "Take it easy, very good," as Pasang used to say.

I have known two generations of Sherpas, and although they have changed in one or two respects, they are still the same delightful companions they have always been. In the old days they were provided by the Himalayan Club, and the sahib-Sherpa relationship was a gentleman's agreement. Nowadays they are organized in trade unions which protect their rights and safeguard their earnings but are always coming up against one another. A Sherpa from Darjeeling, for instance, may not work in Nepal, and the days when Sherpas operated in the far-off Karakorum are over. In the old days they wore long pigtails and were steeped in the old traditions; now they are dressed in the most modish Alpine outfits, and many of them have been invited to visit the countries that organized their most successful expeditions. Pasang Dawa Lama, the sirdar (leader) of our Sherpas on the Cho Oyu expedition, later spent a week or two in Austria and Germany, bringing with him his young wife Yang Chin. The wedding had been the high spot of the celebrations of our success, although another wife was waiting for him back in Darjeeling, and some of his sons were already fully fledged Sherpas. As I said just now, Himalayan tabus can hardly be described as strict.

Pasang was an experienced man of the world and the most famous Sherpa of all after Tensing. In 1939 he and the American Fritz Wiessner all but got to the top of the world's second highest mountain, K2 (28,250 feet). Yet back in her native village south of Mount Everest his wife Yang Chin had never even seen a wheel. The two arrived by air and viewed the wonders of the Western world without turning a hair. As soon as they arrived in Vienna, Pasang said he was very disappointed that no press conference had been arranged. Sometimes at lectures he would be asked to start the proceedings with a sentence or two in his own language, and he almost had to be dragged from the microphone by force. He didn't know what stage fright was and reveled in having an audience to talk to. Flying around the tower of St. Stephen's (a stupendous spectacle) in a helicopter, he wanted to know if the machine could fly faster. On the Grossglockner, driving snow and cloud prevented us from reaching the top, and after a snug night in the Hoffmann hut he complained of drafts and rheumatic pains. Yet on Cho Oyu he had spent a night at 23,000 feet wrapped only in a tarpaulin. At a reception in the Vienna City Hall he pronounced the sherry to be "as sweet as sugarwater." So the hospitable burgomaster ordered him to be brought a large glass of slivovitz. Pasang took to it at once and was all for following the old Sherpa custom of pouring the rest of the fiery liquid down the burgomaster's throat, whereupon the burgomaster observed that he could well understand one had to be pretty tough to go on a Himalaya expedition.

Pasang's brother Ang Nima was the most sensitive Sherpa I have ever known, and as our cook he used to suffer agonies. Being an expedition's cook is not the easiest of jobs at the best of times. At every meal he would subject us all to an anxious scrutiny, and unless our faces lit up after the first mouthful, his eyes would fill with tears.

The Sherpas are very observant and very good at summing up their "sahibs." Most of them had a poor opinion of H. W. Tilman and Eric Shipton, whose ascetic way of life and lack of interest in food were not at all popular. "Very strong, very fast—but no sugar in the tea" was the universal complaint. The Japanese, on the other hand, were highly thought of: "They give you plenty to eat and drink."

Whenever an expedition looks as if it is becoming strenuous, the Sherpas' enthusiasm will flag noticeably, and they will start thinking of their families and their futures. Ang Tharke, the sirdar who accompanied the French expedition on the first conquest of a 26,000-footer, Annapurna, tells how "in Camp V the sahibs asked me if I wanted to go on with them to the top. I said no, my shoes were a bit tight and I was afraid my toes would get frostbitten." When the summit party proposed to assault the peak with a minimum of gear, Ang Tharke gave them a solemn warning: "If you go up without tents and sleeping-bags you and the sahibs will all die. Leave the food behind by all means, you can go for a day or two without food, but you can't survive up there without sleeping-bags." When Maurice Herzog and Louis Lachenal returned to camp after reaching the summit, they were badly frostbitten, and "we had to carry them the whole way back. They were as helpless as children and couldn't do anything for themselves at all. We even had to feed and dress them. We were terribly sorry for them: they were good sahibs and always saw to it that we were properly looked after."

Another Sherpa, Phensing, proudly related how in Katmandu "we lived in the Maharajah's house. The Maharajah presented the Sahib with two large medals, but the medals couldn't save the Sahib's toes, poor devil." When reminded that there were plenty of good artificial toes on the market, Phensing replied: "For the sahibs perhaps, but not for us. I'm glad I didn't go on up to the top; if I had, I might never have been able to work again for the rest of my life."

Pasang was not always as prudent as Ang Tharke. On Cho Oyu he threatened to cut his throat if the Swiss expedition got to the top first. His throat was not cut.

The most serious-minded Sherpa I ever had to do with was Kitar, who accompanied me on a "forbidden" expedition to Tibet and on the summit of Gurla Mandatha (25,500 feet) kept invoking his gods. He was an experienced Sherpa with an Everest expedition to his credit, and on Merkl's ill-fated German assault on Nanga Parbat he could hardly be prevailed upon to abandon his dying sahibs. He was very proud of his German Red Cross medal.

Whenever the wind died down, he would indulge in family reminiscences, or rather expectations, in which his wife played a steadily diminishing role and his unborn son featured more and more prominently. He never doubted for a moment that the child would be a boy and would one day be a famous Sherpa, perhaps even a "tiger." When we had to turn back just below the summit, he comforted himself with the reflection that although the conditions had been too much for us, his son would one day make the summit.

When we got back to civilization, Kitar found a letter waiting for him. He had it read to him in the bazaar, and it confirmed his conviction: It was a boy. But Kitar never lived to see his son. Without returning home, he joined the British Nanda Devi (25,793 feet) expedition and perished.

Fifteen years later I was in Darjeeling and met Kitar's son. Kitar's confident prophecy came back to me: "We were forced to turn back, but he will go on to the top." The son standing in front of me was a gnomelike hunchback.

96

69 A porter on a pass leading to the Langtrang Valley, Nepal

"I knew your father well," I said. "We were good friends."

"Ah," replied the gnome and gave me a shy glance.

"Your father was a great tiger," I tried again.

He smiled and said nothing.

Then I remembered the letter telling Kitar of the "happy event." It was a long letter and written in Hindustani. I tried to find out who had written the letter and what details had been withheld in the reading. But fifteen years are a long time: Kitar's wife, the gnome's mother, was dead, and there was nothing more to be learned.

Kitar told me about the birth of his son as if it were a matter of course. But perhaps the letter had contained details of the deformed child; in which case, was it pride or bitter disappointment that led him to conceal the true facts from me? And how did he die? In the certainty that his son would follow in his footsteps in the regions of eternal snow and scale the most glittering heights of all? Or in the abject despondency of a man whose way through life comes to its lonely end?

I do not know: but I often think of Kitar.

Yak and Yeti

The yak and the yeti (abominable snowman) are as much a part of a Sherpa's life as an igloo is of an Eskimo's—or so we fondly imagine. In point of fact there are many Eskimos who have never set foot inside an igloo, and there is no Sherpa who can produce really convincing evidence of having actually *seen* a yeti. Since potatoes were introduced and the Tibetan frontier was closed, many Sherpas have abandoned their nomadic existence, which means that yaks are no longer a vital necessity.

Nevertheless, the yak *(Bos grunniens)* is still the most important domestic animal in the Himalayas and adjoining Tibet. Yaks are a sort of mountain cattle, usually bigger and stronger then European cattle, with long, shaggy hair which gives them a fearsome appearance. They do not enjoy altitudes below 11,500 feet above sea level, and yak caravans from Tibet have to transfer the loads onto other beasts of burden. A yak can provide pretty well everything its owner needs. Its milk, which contains more fat than cow's milk, is made into butter and cheese. The butter and the dried cheese that looks and feels like sugar candy are staple items in every Himalayan home. Yak meat tastes good and can be half dried or smoked in the open air. Yak hair is used to make carpets, materials, and ropes. At treeless altitudes yak's dung is the only available fuel. Yaks' tails are used as adornments and fly whisks, and their tendons and intestines can be used in all sorts of ways. Like the Masai in East Africa, the Sherpas have also found a way of getting nourishment out of a yak without slaughtering it: Blood drained from the carotid artery makes succulent sausages and a specialty that tastes rather like grilled liver. As if all this were not enough, the yak is an extremely tough beast of burden and an excellent climber, making light of loads of up to 275 pounds on even the roughest tracks. Its popularity in the Himalayas is hardly surprising, especially since it is the principal means of transportation in the entire area: Horses and mules cannot manage the high passes, and the sheep and goats which are often used as beasts of burden in the western Himalayas can carry loads of only between 45 and 65 pounds. Moreover, sheep are much more affected by adverse weather conditions than the more robust yaks. I once had a harrowing experience with a sheep caravan on the Mana Pass in the Garwhal Himalayas. Just below the summit there was rain, and the animals got wet to the skin. Shortly afterward the caravan ran into a snowstorm, and after becoming encased in a coating of ice, the wretched animals collapsed from sheer exhaustion. The next morning I counted thirty-six dead sheep littering this *via dolorosa*.

For all its toughness the yak is a sensitive creature and is distinctly recalcitrant if roughly handled. Loading a yak in a rebellious mood requires a lot of patience, and to try to mount one is just asking for trouble. Yaks are steered and kept going by volleys of stones right, left and behind (but not direct hits). The effect of the stones is augmented by various manifestations of the human voice—whistling, singing, tongue clicking, sighing, yodeling, and snorting. Every yak driver has his own favorite method, but since whistling is the usual one, it is an unpardonable social blunder to whistle in a Sherpa household—it means you want the occupants to move on.

Faced with having to cross an ice-cold river with yaks, the novice is often tempted to do so on the animal's back, because even in a torrent that would carry a man away like a piece of wood yaks can keep a foothold, and they are strong swimmers, too. The only drawback—in my experience at any rate—is that a yak takes umbrage at his extra burden and deliberately submerges. Instead of getting wet up to the thighs, as is usually the case, the rider is soaked to the neck, and since most of the rivers where yaks come from are ice-cold glacier water, one soon learns to cross them on foot rather than astride a yak.

Unlike other Himalayan peoples, the Sherpas are good cattle breeders and cross yaks with Nepal cattle. The female offspring, known as zhum, are fertile and yield more milk than pure-blooded cows. The male offspring, zopkio, cannot reproduce themselves but make excellent beasts of burden. Incidentally, there is no such thing as yak milk, because a female yak is known as a nak, so that the proper name for the excellent creamy drink she provides is nak milk.

Northern Nepal's agricultural exports used to go to Tibet, which needed butter for the lamps in the monasteries and for blending with tea. But Communism first extinguished the lamps and then closed the frontiers. It was the Swiss who offered the Nepalese a solution. In the Langtrang Valley, a rich yak pasturage, they established what must be the highest cheese dairy in the world. At first it was hard going, but in due course the Swiss taught the local Nepalese farmers how to produce an "Emmentaler" that is every bit as good as the Swiss original. The cheese is then transported to Katmandu (a seven-day walk, although the Katmandu–Lhasa motor road will make a world of difference) and from there exported to various neighboring countries. The success of this Swiss initiative has been prodigious. With the minimum of outlay and no political strings attached, it has helped the Nepalese build up a thriving trade that can be expanded to all their mountain valleys, quite apart from the profits it brings in for the farmers and the foreign exchange for the country as a whole.

And God knows Nepal certainly needs all the foreign exchange it can get. While impoverished, half-starved India can boast a yearly income of about $65 a head, the corresponding figure for Nepal is $40. Nepal has no mineral deposits to export and hardly any fruit. So cheese could become the country's principal industrial export.

Nepal's oddest and most elusive source of foreign exchange is the yeti, which seldom, if ever, puts in an appearance. As in the case of the Loch Ness monster, there is no knowing whether it really exists, and Himalayan experts are divided into two camps, those who believe in the yeti and those who do not. The yeti first cropped up about the turn of the century in the form of reports of a biped that was not a human being but looked like one. The first real yeti sensation came in 1951, when on the Merling Pass, at a height of just under 20,000 feet, Eric Shipton photographed distinct yeti footprints in soft snow. The tracks were unmistakably those of a biped with five toes. Each footprint was about nine feet long and six inches broad, and the stride was about the same as that of an adult human being. Up to that time the yeti had existed only in the yarns and hallucinations of half-exhausted mountaineers, but here was a photograph, objective and indisputable.

In our part of the world the yeti is a synonym for the "abominable snowman," but this highly derogatory expression is in fact due to a mistranslation, the Tibetan word for "demon" having been mistranslated as "abominable." The word "yeti" is a compound of ye, rock, and teh, animal— "rock animal." But the natives of the Himalayas have different names for the creature, depending on the size of the animal and the nature of the local dialect, such as mi-teh (an animal that looks like a man or an anthropoid ape), or kang-mi (snowman), or dzu-teh (cattle animal, the yeti being said to have a predilection for beef). Many Sherpas claim to have encountered yetis, and are only too glad to give a vivid and voluble account of their appalling experience. But pressed for details, they have to admit that they themselves have never actually seen one, but that a neighbor or an uncle had (invariably someone who had left the neighborhood or was no longer alive).

Some Sherpas even claim to have once captured a yeti that came down to their village every evening and drank from the trough. The villagers were so frightened that they barricaded themselves in their houses, but after the yeti had gone, they filled the trough with strong chang. The next morning they found a completely intoxicated yeti snoring off his potations. At the sight of this pathetic spectacle their fears evaporated, and they were immediately struck by the business possibilities of the situation. Remembering how keen the white sahibs were to catch a yeti, they bound the creature's hands and feet and carried him down the valley slung on a pole. On the second day the yeti emerged from his stupor, broke his bonds, killed one of the Sherpas, and vanished into the realms of legend.

A more romantic and less unedifying tale is that of the young Sherpa girl who was abducted by a yeti and did not return to her village for several weeks. She is said to have preserved a discreet silence on what actually happened to her, although every now and then a smile would flit across her face. But even this firsthand authority on a yeti's life was invariably living somewhere else or had gone on a long journey whenever a sahib wanted to get some information out of her.

One cold, damp night Adjiba, one of my best Sherpa friends, surprised me by producing some marvelously dry brushwood out of his rucksack. Although it was freezing cold, he refused to use

Sven Hedin being attacked by a ferocious yak. "Its breath belched from its nostrils like clouds of steam and its snout was almost touching the ground. It was about to impale its victims on its horns, toss them into the air, and then trample them to pulp with its forelegs. As it came nearer and nearer I could hear it snorting and blowing like a steam-saw. Turning in my saddle I perceived that the beast was within about 20 yards of me. I could see its small glinting eyes ablaze with insensate fury as the creature rolled them till their whites were bloodshot. It was a matter of seconds now. I was on the extreme right, so that I and my horse would be the first to be gored. The horses flexed their legs like bowstrings. I took off my red bashlik and waved it in front of the yak to distract its attention." (From *Transhimalaya* by Sven Hedin, Leipzig, 1909)

it, however. When I pressed him for a reason, he said it was yeti wood with a smell that the abominable snowman could not abide, so that if we were threatened by a yeti, the smell of the wood would keep him off. In other aspects Adjiba is a pretty level-headed guy, yet he would rather freeze than "waste" any of his yeti wood. Unfortunately, during the whole four months of our expedition we never once had occasion to put the wood to the test.

Despite their commonsense attitude to everyday life in general, and the perils of mountaineering in particular, Sherpas are very fond of colorful stories. Their patron saint, Lama Sanga Dorje, is said to have been able to fly by using his lama's cloak as wings and to have hung out his washing on the rays of sunshine that penetrated a dark room. So there was nothing extraordinary about finding desiccated yetis' scalps in some Sherpa monasteries. Although they were not revered as sacred relics, there was considerable reluctance to exhibit them to strangers. They had thick skins and russet brown hair and were not like the scalps of any known animal. The priests said they had been in the monastery since time immemorial.

In the 1950's the yeti soared to the zenith of his fame. Now that all the peaks of 25,000 feet and more had been conquered, the Himalayas were no longer news. But for the yeti, or rather for the yeti hunters, any amount of financial backing was forthcoming. The London *Daily Mail* and the American oil millionaire Tom Slick were among those who financed yeti expeditions. By this time Nepal had nationalized the yeti, and it was illegal to kill one or smuggle one out of the country. All yeti rights were owned by the government, and a tax of about $600 was levied on all yeti expeditions. These expeditions were very thoroughly organized and prepared, complete with nets, hounds, and narcotic missiles. Even learned anthropologists were roped in. The strategy was to stupefy the yeti with narcotic missiles, photograph, weigh, and measure him while he was unconscious, subject him to a thorough medical examination, and then let him go "with a puzzled expression on his face and a plaster on his behind" as one intrepid yeti hunter put it. The expeditions hoped that the yeti would prove to be the missing link.

One can endeavor to relate the origin of human life in Asia to the expansion of the Himalayas during the last 600,000 years. The forests were unable to withstand the increasing cold, and the apes were obliged to go on two feet if they were to survive. The Peking man discovered not far from the Chinese capital was familiar with fire and used rudimentary tools. But it is possible that the missing link still exists in some inaccessible part of the Himalayas. What a chance for anthropologists to demonstrate the development of man by a living creature instead of fossils!

To anticipate for a moment—although none of these expeditions ever set eyes on an abominable snowman, they at least confirmed the suspicions that he exists. Sir Edmund Hillary took the scalp from Khumjung monastery on a tour of Europe and America for expert examination; it turned out to be a 200- to 300-year-old fake from a bear. Even Hillary, a notable benefactor of the Sherpas, who in his quiet way showed his gratitude by building them schools and hospitals, had a job to get permission to "export" the scalp. Two conditions were that it must be returned to the monastery by a definite date (this entailed the chartering of a helicopter) and that the oldest man in the village must accompany it on its overseas journey. The latter expressed his readiness with typical Sherpa assurance, and since it was put to him that in the course of his travels, he would meet the King of Nepal, the Queen of England, and the President of the United States, he set out, with appropriate presents: tea and tsamba, dried yaks' tails, and paintings on parchment.

The disappointment over the scalps not being relics of some unknown creature was compensated for by other discoveries. In addition to the tracks in the snow, tracks were found in damp earth, and plaster casts were made of them. Furthermore, yeti excrement shows that the creature lives on plants and smaller animals; in other words, it is omnivorous. And a yeti nest was made of shrubs that the strongest Sherpa could not uproot.

The figment that yetis sometimes go backward to throw hunters off their track is easily explained. When walking erect on two legs, anthropoid apes use their hands to help themselves along, and the imprints of the hands on the ground point the wrong way.

It should be remembered that the Nepalese side of the Mount Everest area is called Mahalangur-Himan, "the snowy mountains of the great ape," a proof that the existence of this creature has been known for a long, long time.

102

The misleading term "snowman" is due to the first tracks having been found on snow and glaciers. The yeti, like the chamois, lives below the snow line, but sometimes it has to cross expanses of snow, and this is when it is spotted. So the question of what a yeti can be doing on a glacier is superfluous. As a British mountaineer put it: "The yeti will probably ask us the same question."

Among some of the more fanciful fables about yetis is that they are descendants of Tibetan criminals living in exile in the Himalayas or of hermits who found out the secret of immortality and ran wild. Tales of this kind are laughed out of court by Himalayan experts, but nearly all the great mountaineers—Hunt, Hillary, Günter Dyhrenfurth, George C. Band, to name only a few—believe implicitly in the existence of an unknown creature of some kind. "It would be nice if the Himalayas could keep at least one secret to themselves."

Personally I only once came across tracks of the "abominable snowman," and that was on Nar Parbat in the Garhwal Himalayas, one of the easier mountains. I had only one Sherpa, Nima, with me, and I was the only European for miles around. Suddenly, there were the tracks on a glacier, and Nima said, "Yeti." The tracks looked as if they were about two days old and were beginning to melt. They started in scree, went winding across the glacier, carefully avoiding snow-covered crevasses, and disappeared in the scree the other side of the glacier. They were rather like the tracks of an old man short of breath who was constantly on the point of sinking into deep snow. We camouflaged ourselves in white sheets and spent two days trying to get a photograph of the mysterious creature. There could not have been any other climber in the neighborhood, and this particular mountain was not one that the locals made a habit of climbing, all the more so because in places it requires crampons and ice axes. I went back to the next village, Mana, and interrogated the inhabitants about whether anyone had been on Nar Parbat recently. They shook their heads, and Nethar Singh, a tall Bhutia who had been on one or two expeditions and was looked up to as a positive globe-trotter by the rest of the villagers, said, "I know why you ask; you've seen yeti tracks." He added that the British climber Frank Smythe had also found yeti tracks in the same place. He

The popular idea of a yeti

had mobilized fifty men and conducted an exhaustive search, but in vain. "Yeti very timid," said Nima, an opinion with which anyone who has ever tried to track down this elusive creature will heartily agree.

Yeti tracks are nearly always found in the central and eastern Himalayas, but as soon as the yeti became news, reports came pouring in from all over the place. But as far as I know no yeti has ever been heard of in the Karakorum.

In Chitral there is another legendary creature, the "glacier frog." It is about the size of a calf, has the shape of a frog, and lives in glacier crevasses. What it lives on, nobody seems to know. Many people who claim to have seen one, usually indistinctly silhouetted against the background of a crevasse, maintain that its head and back were encrusted in gold and diamonds.

An Indian pilgrim who was not at all of a mystical turn of mind (in fact he was a railroad engineer) told me a similar story about a king cobra that was alleged to infest the mountains near Badrinath. The creature's head was said to be covered in diamonds worth a fortune, and at immense length the Indian told me the secret of how to get hold of them without succumbing to the serpent's venomous vigilance. Ordinary methods were of no avail at all, but when the moon was full, the creature could be induced by magic rites and carefully prescribed ritual—I forget the exact details—to slough off the diamonds, which could then be appropriated without further ado. As a token of gratitude the cobra should be presented with a saucer of warm goat's milk. In due course I became quite an expert on king cobras, but unfortunately I never had an opportunity of turning the Indian's secret to account.

The Islamic Chitralis were more down to earth. They had little use for rites and incantations; to capture a glacier frog, more drastic measures were necessary. A smith, who was a shrewd enough businessman to have earned enough money to buy himself a truck, suggested we should go into partnership: He would make the right kind of fishhook, and if I managed to catch a glacier frog with it, we should go fifty-fifty on the proceeds. To avoid losing face and appearing a complete sucker, I stuck out for a bigger share for myself; after all, it was I who was exposing myself to the perils of frog fishing. But for some reason or other our scheme never came off. Nevertheless I was very grateful to the glacier frog. In those days the Chitralis were still backwoodsmen, so to speak, and had nothing of the Sherpas' experience of anything so crazy as mountaineering. To the

104

71

72

73

74

75

76

77

78

79

Chitralis I was an inexplicable phenomenon and was consequently viewed with mistrust. But once the news got around that I was after a glacier frog, they gave me enthusiastic support. Obviously I was a get-rich-quick type, far too smart a guy to let myself in for any laborious drudgery.

Despite their rather ferocious appearance and the inevitable gun that they carry around like a favorite toy (or so one hoped), the hospitality of the Chitralis and their neighbors the Kohistanis is overwhelming. Overwhelming in the truest sense of the word, and for the newcomer somewhat unnerving. My first experience of it was at a place called Gabrial near the Indus River. I had left my companions far behind when I was suddenly confronted on a narrow track by two desperate-looking characters. We were unable to converse in any language, but they had the usual gun, and I had an enticingly bulging rucksack. They pointed to the ground—the three of us were to have a little rest together. I complied, and the next minute they had torn my rucksack off my shoulders and laid me out flat on the ground. Then they both started in on me, and I remember wondering why they didn't just take the rucksack and make off. Instead, they started to massage me. One applied himself to my upper half, and the other got to work on my legs. They were immensely strong and showed nothing of the ordinary sauna masseur's concern for his victim's comfort. Sometimes I was sure they were going to break every bone in my body, as well as tear my muscles to shreds. With their bare feet they trampled on my chest, my back, and my thighs, their toes digging deep into my flesh. By the time they had finished with me my body was one big ache, yet half an hour later I felt like a new man, fresh and invigorated.

In the end I got properly hooked on this treatment. It is frequently handed out as a gesture of welcome, to new arrivals in a village, for instance. But for the donors it is a distinctly strenuous business, and to get them to keep it up, one has to give something in return. It was in this way that I ran through nearly all my priceless tobacco—not that I regretted it for a moment. If ever I return to this desolate Indus-Kohistan part of the world, it will be mainly to feel horny Chitrali feet trampling all over my prostrate body.

The Unknown Himalayas

The farther east you go, the more "unknown" the Himalayas become. Nepal has been thoroughly explored, and all its peaks have been climbed. The same applies to Sikkim, which before the opening up of Nepal was a mountaineer's paradise and could boast the "world's most beautiful mountain," Siniolchu. Bhutan, on the other hand, is still inaccessible, and only a handful of Westerners have ever been allowed to set foot in it. Nor have there ever been any major mountaineering expeditions to Bhutan. Admittedly the 23,000-foot Chomo Lhari, on the frontier between Nepal and Bhutan, was climbed in 1937, but from the Tibetan side. The vast territory known as the North East Frontier Agency (NEFA), circumscribing the Brahmaputra River like an immense horseshoe and stretching right up to the Burma frontier, is of no strategic or economic importance and was therefore neglected by the British. The various tribes there still eke out their traditional existence. The dense, swampy jungle and high mountains are daunting obstacles to the spread of civilization, and the only people who have been able to bring back reports of what is probably the most ethnologically interesting part of the Himalayas have been one or two explorers and government officials. But in recent years three important events have put the NEFA on the map, so to speak. In 1955 the Nagas rebelled, and their demand for independence led to protracted hostilities. It was here too that in 1959 the Dalai Lama set foot on Indian soil on his flight from Lhasa. A year or two later came the fighting between India and China, and an invasion of Assam seemed imminent. History has shown that the Himalayas are by no means an insurmountable barrier. On the contrary, an aggressor from the north enjoys excellent lines of approach and communication, and since the Chinese are highly efficient road builders, they can assemble troops and material at will. The defenders, on the other hand, are at the terrible disadvantage of having to fight uphill (and the Himalayan passes are exceedingly steep).

Ask any expert on the Himalayas where he would choose to settle permanently, and in all probability he will reply, "Sikkim." This tiny kingdom of about 2,700 square miles and with a population of 160,000 offers more beauty and variety than any other part of the Himalayas, with the possible exception of the Valley of Nepal. But whereas at Katmandu the giant mountains are a remote, though spectacular, background, the whole of Sikkim is dominated by its sacred mountain, Kanchenjunga. The name means "the five treasures of eternal snow" or "the great glacier of the five treasures." The Tibetan god of wealth chose its peak as his abode and hoarded his treasures there: gold, silver, precious stones, wheat, and sacred books. The Lepchas, the original inhabitants of Sikkim, also have a fine and appropriate name for the mountain: "the loftiest veil of ice."

Before World War II, there were two unsuccessful expeditions to Kanchenjunga. In 1955 the British were given permission to organize an expedition, but the Indian, Nepalese, and Sikkim authorities requested them to call it off, because a violation of the sacred mountain would have grave consequences. The British respected the plea and promised not to set foot on the summit. True to their word, they turned back 10 feet below the top. They entitled their book on the expedition *The Untrodden Summit*, a gesture that was appreciated by Buddhists and Hindus alike.

For the faithful, sacred mountains are strictly off limits. The Sherpa Kitar who accompanied me to Tibet, and gave such a heroic account of himself on Gurla Mandhata, could only stare at me in amazement when I allowed myself the observation that the sacred Mount Kailas presented no difficulties and could easily be conquered via the east ridge. In his view, the very idea of climbing it was sacrilege, and no amount of coaxing or threatening would have induced him to have anything to do with such an enterprise. And if I had tried to go it alone, he would probably have reported me to the authorities.

That sacred mountains are no joke was something I learned in the Garhwal Himalayas. The local shepherds revered a mountain close to the frontier which was simply asking to be climbed and promised a superb view from its summit. I could never find out what was so sacred about this mountain; I can record only that Nima refused point-blank to have anything to do with climbing it. No good would come of it. However, one day there was a cloudless sky, and the air was so clear that I could not resist the temptation to enjoy a view of Tibet from the summit of Kailas, which dominates the surrounding countryside. All of Nima's attempts to deter me from this blasphemous undertaking were in vain. After all, it was such a lovely day. But the "lovely day" didn't last very long. I was still a long way from the summit when the clouds came up from the valleys and enveloped me in an icy gray pall. Soon I was being lashed by gigantic hailstones, and unable to find a single hospitable rock behind which to shelter, I beat an ignominious retreat. Back at our camp Nima gave me a broad grin and positively enjoyed telling me that down at the camp there had not been a spot of rain the whole day (and indeed the earth was bone-dry). Yet the mountain was still swathed in a great black cloud that was like a warning to stop frivolously desecrating the realms of the gods. I also remembered a superstition attaching to the Thui Pass near Gilgit: If anyone came to grief on it, it would remain wrapped in cloud for three days, for that was the time the soul took to make its way to heaven. I repeated this legend to Nima, and he regarded it as only natural that even in the far-off mountains of Pakistan the gods should be all-powerful and welcome the dead with ceremony.

For some days Nima's attitude to me was distinctly reserved, until an omen (in which I had a hand) reassured him that the gods had forgiven me. In pouring rain and soaked to the skin, we arrived late one evening at a tiny village. Perhaps there was really no room in the village, or perhaps the villagers were just in an unfriendly mood; at all events, all they offered us was a goat sty which was too low to stand up in and so muddy that there was not even a dry spot for our rucksacks. However, I managed to make a sort of bed out of some boards just under the roof; it was uncomfortable, but at least dry. It also had the advantage of ensuring that one's face could not be trodden on by a goat. Nima, who had once been a shepherd, was quite unmoved by the proximity of the animals and managed to make himself at home in a convenient corner. After drinking gallons of tea, we turned in, and inevitably the exigencies of nature soon made themselves felt. But what with the cold mud and the goats' excrement I did not relish the idea of getting out of "bed," so I relieved myself from where I was. The next morning I had forgotten the whole thing, the rain had stopped, the mountains were covered in dazzling new snow, and Nima had never been in such sparkling form. Obviously he had forgiven my impiety. During a halt at a place with a breathtaking view he came clean: He was sure the gods were well disposed to us now, so we could have a go at even the most difficult mountains—all would go well. I asked him what made him so sure. He said that during the night the roof of the goat sty had leaked, and no matter how many times he changed his position, the rain kept dripping on him, and it was freezing cold, as well as wet. All at once a miracle happened: The rain was warm, and this was a sign from the gods that they were well disposed. I was too ashamed to attempt an explanation and puncture Nima's confidence.

Another thing Nima told me was that the only way of bagging a snow grouse with stones was to subject the stones to special treatment beforehand. My only excuse for embarking on such an unedifying subject is that we were very hungry and the grouse were succulently fat and very tame. But we never seemed to hit them, although Nima had several near-misses. I asked him how he could explain such murderous activities, seeing that his religion forbade killing animals. He laughed: Snow grouse and stones were the same color and lived on the same mountain; therefore, they were brothers and could not possibly do each other any harm. So it was impossible, I asked, to kill these birds with a stone? Not necessarily, Nima replied, only the stone must be subjected to indignities and made angry so that it would forget its fraternal affinity. Apparently not all stones had the same temperament. With some, it was enough just to spit on them; others had to be defiled by urine.

When I said I didn't believe it, Nima proceeded to convert one or two substantial stones into lethal weapons. Maybe the grouse spotted that the stones were moist and that operations had now taken a more serious turn; at all events they flew away.

The "untrodden summit" of "the five treasures of eternal snow" has led us into the realms of belief and superstition, so back to the tiny kingdom of Sikkim.

Nobody knows where Sikkim's original inhabitants, the amiable Lepchas, came from. Racially and linguistically they are akin to the Tibetans, meaning that they probably came down to the "land of rice" over the high passes to the north. In the Sikkim language, which is being increasingly ousted by Nepali, the country is called the Land of Caves and its inhabitants are the Brothers of Bamboo, bamboo being the most important material in their day-to-day lives. Their forebears were created by a god out of the ice of Kanchenjunga; that is why it is a sacred mountain.

The Lepchas cherish two legends that are so like the Biblical stories of the Flood and the Tower of Babel that in all probability they were propagated here by the first missionaries, but their origin is far earlier. It seems that long, long ago the land was submerged under a terrible flood. One Himalayan peak after another disappeared from view, and everyone was drowned except one couple who had sought safety on the summit of Tendong, the "Exalted Horn," which is actually one of the smaller mountains (a mere 8,780 feet). The gods allowed it to shoot up during the flood, however, so the pair survived. But like the inmates of Noah's Ark, the first they knew of their good fortune was when a bird flew past with a twig in its beak.

One day the Lepchas decided to build such a huge tower that from the top of it they would be able to grab the sky with a hook. For their building material they chose earthenware pots, and the workmen were divided into three classes: those who made the pots, those who transported them, and those who piled them on top of one another. Work went ahead so rapidly that in next to no time the topmost workers were almost touching the sky, so they called down to the others to send them up a bent bough so that they could hook down the sky. But the message was misunderstood, and the people below thought the tower was finished and that they were to destroy the earthenware pots, and this they did. The tower collapsed, hundreds of workers were buried under the rubble, and the survivors were no longer able to make themselves understood in conversation. The scene of this legendary disaster is now a rice field on which earthenware fragments are constantly being dug up.

The earliest historical information about Sikkim goes back to the mid-seventeenth century when Tibetan domination was established by a noble family who still rule the country. The kings of Sikkim and their wives are notable for their aristocratic features, abundant charm, and high standard of civilization. The national religion is Buddhism, and Sikkim's links with Tibet were always closer than Nepal's—that is until the Chinese arrived in Lhasa.

112

80 A mani (praying) wall near Mount Everest

In 1963 the present Maharajah Kumar Palden Thondup Namgyal married a twenty-three-year-old American student from New York, following six months of deliberations between Sikkim and the government of India on the possible religious and political repercussions of such a union. The answer has been—apparently none. The student, the only American woman except Princess Grace of Monaco to occupy a throne, was converted to Buddhism, adopted the becoming national costume, cultivated the graceful movements of her new compatriots, and learned their melodious language. Visitors to Sikkim's capital, Gangtok, who have been fortunate enough to be allowed to see her, have invariably raved about her.

Sikkim's easterly neighbor is the principality of Bhutan, officially known as Druk-yul, Land of the Dragon. For a long time it was ruled jointly by a temporal deb raja and a spiritual dharma raja, but the local chieftains (penlops), who owned strongholds (dzongs) in nine different valleys, pursued their own individual policies and fought one another almost incessantly. Eventually the Penlop of Tongsa came out on top and became the hereditary maharaja (gyalpo).

In earlier times Bhutan was ruled by a Hindu maharaja, but in the eighth century it was converted to Buddhism by a magician named Pamasambhava. During a period of meditation in eastern Bhutan he leaned against a rock; the mark can still be seen and is preserved as a sacred relic.

While Nepal is an independent state and Sikkim is a protectorate of India, Bhutan enjoys a status, halfway between the two, which is rather difficult to define. Defense and foreign policy are looked after by Delhi, but Bhutan still has "full autonomy in domestic affairs" and has developed a kind of grass-root democracy. Modern ideas are being administered to Bhutan in small doses, to pave the way, without impairing the country's ancient and individual structure, for a kind of democracy that will slowly but surely infiltrate the traditional social order.

Bhutan's independence is attested by its membership in the World Postal Union and the Colombo Plan and by the United States having set its immigration quota on a par with India's 400 immigrants a year. Actually, no one is yet known to have emigrated from Bhutan.

The present ruler has initiated agricultural reforms and built many hospitals and roads. His ambition is to ensure that every male child has a chance of attending school (voluntarily or compulsorily) without having to make his way there through a jungle in which he may well be set upon by leeches. In all probability this ambition will be fulfilled a good deal earlier than expected. Owing to the tension between India and China, there can be no vacuum in the Himalayas; it will very soon be filled.

If, as I said just now, Sikkim would be the pleasantest of the Himalayan countries to settle in, Bhutan is certainly the strangest. The highly colored garments favored by the men look like Japanese kimonos, and the bow-and-arrow competitions that are the national sport would not be out of place on another planet.

The least-known Himalayan country is the North East Frontier Agency (NEFA), which has 650,000 inhabitants and is about the same size as Austria. The mountains are lower, and the only peaks over 23,000 feet—Kangdu and Namcha Barwa—both are in Tibet. The first encounters between the British and the natives were punitive expeditions to spoil the latter's appetite for incursions into the fertile plains. The natives proved to be distrustful, disciplined, and courageous, with a passion for head hunting that led them to massacre expeditions to the last man. It was therefore decided to leave them in peace as long as they did not erupt from their mountains too often.

An even greater deterrent than the ferocity of the natives is the climate. The monsoon lasts from May till October, and the annual average rainfall amounts in some areas to 240 inches. For ethnologists most of the NEFA is an almost hopeless proposition. Its 650,000 inhabitants include no fewer than eighteen different tribes, such as the Monpa, Sherdukpen, Dafla, Apotani, Abor, Mishmi, Kampti, and Naga. There are forty-four different languages and dialects, and the inhabitants of a valley are very often unable to understand neighbors living within shotgun range. Some are Buddhists, and others profess an obscure form of Hinduism; but the majority have adhered to the faith of their forefathers. They believe in a life after death and take good care to keep on the right side of departed spirits by laying offerings on their graves. The only tribe I have had personal experience of is the Mishmi, whose members are reserved but hospitable. One particular habit of theirs which will not endear them to foreigners is their predilection for eating live beetles, caterpillars, and worms, which they carry around with them in their haversacks. One does not exactly look forward to being invited to a meal; misunderstandings are more than probable.

The Search for Shangri-La

The Himalayan peoples regard themselves as one big brotherhood. It is as if they shared the same native land, to which they owed a common debt of gratitude for all the wonders it has to offer and an allegiance that neither time nor distance can weaken. Wherever and whenever I have met a European, an American, or an Australian who has been in the Himalayas or even a Sherpa who has begun a new life in one of the cities of India, we have started to exchange reminiscences of the Himalayas, forgetting all about our environment, our worries, and even our origins. I remember only a single exception, and that was in Basutoland in Africa (which since gaining independence has called itself Lesotho and which, on account of a mountain about 13,000 feet high, is often referred to as the African Switzerland). I was collecting material for a book and at the time was in the hospital, where one afternoon I met Earl C. Denman. A Canadian by birth, he was living in South Africa and was well known for his lone attempt on Everest and for his book *Alone to Everest*. In 1947 he made his way to Tibet without a permit and in disguise. He had acquired previous experience of mountaineering in Africa and possessed a strong will and considerable powers of endurance. With only two Sherpas (one of them was Tensing, who later shared the glory of being the first to climb Everest) and a minimum of equipment, he reached the southern slopes of Everest, although some stages were negotiated only at the second attempt. Yet although snow conditions were ideal, Denman was forced to abandon his attempt to reach the summit. To attempt any peak over 25,000 feet without a sleeping bag is asking for trouble. Denman's account did not tally with Tensing's on all points, but it seems that Denman, who was a fanatical individualist, got to a height of somewhere between

115

21,000 and 23,000 feet before being forced to turn back by the cold. His attempt must go down as a record as regards speed, self-discipline, and perhaps foolhardiness. But I knew nothing of all this when we met, and the hospital doctor only said, "You two will get on fine together; you're both Himalayan people."

Denman achieved a magnificent solo performance, yet there was not a particle of enjoyment in his account of it—no memories, for instance, of the twilight when the topmost peaks still glow above the onset of night lower down. After talking for an hour or two, we separated, and I never saw Denman again. But I often think of him. How was it that the superb Himalayan scenery could leave him with unpleasant memories? Even people who get severely frostbitten in the Himalayas merely smile when reminded of their ordeal or when talking about it. Perhaps Denman had his eyes only on the goal and overlooked the beauty of the approach to it, which, after all, is the same whether one reaches one's goal or not.

Many mystics and philosophers have maintained that somewhere in the Himalayas there is a kind of Shangri-La from where the "lords and masters" direct human activities. None of the hermits and yogis I met in the Himalayas ever claimed that they had the power of influencing events on earth, though many of them had attained a high degree of perfection. But during World War II I did meet in Shanghai a man who without a trace of false modesty gave me to understand that he was was one of the "lords and masters," and had just left his Shangri-La to dwell among ordinary mortals. He turned out to be Trebitsch-Lincoln, one of the most adventurous characters of his day. He was born near Budapest and was brought up to be a rabbi, but the peace of a synagogue was not his idea of life. In Hamburg he became a member of the Lutheran Church and then traveled all over the place earning his living in the most extraordinary variety of jobs. In London he was a Member of Parliament. He was in Hungary during the Béla Kun regime and in Germany at the time of the Kapp Putsch. He acted as an adviser to Chinese generals and lived as a Buddhist monk near Peking, before ending up as one of the many individuals without nationality or passport who thronged Shanghai toward the end of the Second World War, when Shanghai was an open harbor and the "home of the homeless."

Ignatius Timotheus Trebitsch-Lincoln had the burning, hypnotic eyes of a fanatic, and at the time his one aim was to stop the war, a task that for a "grand master" ought not (in his opinion) to be too difficult. He sent letters—"messages" he called them—to Roosevelt, Churchill, Hitler, and Mussolini, but never had an answer to any of them. When he started off on foot on his way back to his Shangri-La to devise new methods, his boots were too tight, and his feet got so badly blistered that he had to return to Shanghai. But he still kept talking about the "masters" who were not going to allow the carnage to go on much longer. He eventually died after a stomach operation, as destitute and wretched as an ordinary mortal could be. For all his blazing eyes and the British Secret Service's conviction that he was one of the top spies and "plotters," his propagation of Shangri-La was far from convincing.

A slightly more rewarding quest for Shangri-La a year or two later was that of Miss Christobal Bevan, a theosophist living in Mexico. One night she had a dream in which she was instructed to arrive at her Shangri-La north of the Tsangpo River when the moon was full. After traveling half way around the world, she set out on the last lap with only two Sherpas and without a permit. She had no experience of mountaineering, and her only equipment was a tattered tent and an overcoat. Her incredible feat of endurance can be explained only by sheer indomitable willpower and faith. After leaving Gangtok, this intrepid fifty-year-old visionary crossed a 19,500-foot pass in snow almost up to her neck, sustained a severe injury, and eventually hobbled half-frozen and exhausted into Shigatse, the most important town in Tibet after Lhasa. As soon as the authorities discovered that she had entered the country without a permit, she was politely but firmly turned back. Her extreme disappointment was mitigated by a second dream in which she was given to understand that what had happened was all for the best, and so she departed without bitterness. From a purely physical point of view, too, her performance was a magnificent feat of strength and ingenuity.

Yet there have been travelers who really do seem to have found their Shangri-La and have no intention of returning to the outside world. I heard, for instance, of a Frenchman who ever since World War II had been vainly attempting to get to Lhasa from China. In one of the lama monasteries near the frontier between Tibet and China he encountered a European who had been living there for years as a monk. In passable French the European politely evaded all questions about his origin and about what had led him to adopt his present way of life. He also requested the Frenchman not to tell anyone about him because he wanted to end his days here in peace. Here was one person who had found his Shangri-La.

But dreamers in search of God are not the only people with stories of a secret retreat of pure felicity. Hardheaded mountaineers can also tell a tale or two. Hillary, the first to climb Everest, relates how in a remote valley his Sherpas discovered a cave full of Tibetan skins, rugs, and carpets, as well as a religious book. The cave was nearly 15,000 feet above sea level, and the only explanation was that it had been used as a hiding place by a lama fleeing from the Chinese invaders. It was decided to leave the objects where they were, but Dawa Tensing, a Sherpa who could read and write, got very excited about the religious book and laboriously copied it out before putting it back where he had found it. It was not until the expedition was disbanding that the learned Sherpa explained why he had been so interested in the book. He said it was about the great saint Guru Rimpotche, who converted Nepal and eastern Tibet to Buddhism. According to an ancient legend, the guru established a village of perpetual peace in which his disciples could escape the turmoil of the outside world. The village was somewhere in the Barun Valley, which is where the book was found; but ordinary mortals would never be able to find the way to the village or even set eyes on it. Nor could anyone enter the village of perpetual peace until he had overcome all the obstacles by which Shangri-La is surrounded and had mastered the secret of meditation, partaken of ultimate wisdom, and observed the divine precepts.

It must have been some such longing, amounting to a mystical urge, that inspired the British mountaineer Frank Smythe. In the years before the Second World War he was one of the most successful of the Himalayan pioneers. In 1931, for instance, he got to the top of Kamet, the highest peak that had ever been climbed, and on an Everest expedition he reached a height of 28,400 feet. In 1949 he was preparing another expedition when he succumbed to a mysterious ailment in Darjeeling. Some years later, knowing nothing of the circumstances of his death, I was on my way by ship to India and the Himalayas. One of the passengers was a nurse who was returning from leave in Europe to her hospital in Darjeeling. When she heard that I was going to do some climbing, she expostulated (and with conviction): "What nonsense! You'll either break your neck or your heart."

"Possibly my neck, or even my leg," I replied, "but why my heart?"

"I've known such a case in Darjeeling myself," she explained, and told me how Smythe had been given permission to tackle Kanchenjunga, the third highest mountain in the world and how while he was putting the finishing touches to his preparations in Darjeeling, permission had been withdrawn for political reasons.

"He just died of a broken heart," the nurse went on. "It wasn't a very edifying spectacle either. He lapsed into a profound melancholy and for hours on end did nothing but gaze through a telescope at the white walls of his room, fancying they were Kanchenjunga. Sometimes when the moon was full, he would give us the slip and climb a little hill where there was a better view of the mountain. Eventually he was sent back to England, where he died shortly afterward. Of a broken heart."

I cannot, of course, tell whether the nurse's story accords with the facts or was just a figment of her imagination. I only know that I could not get the expression "a broken heart" out of my mind. Anyone who knows how superb the view from Darjeeling is will have little difficulty in believing the story.

One of Smythe's best books is about a high valley in the Garhwal Himalayas with particularly luxuriant vegetation. I spent some time there while loftier aspirations were blotted out by monsoon rain and lowering clouds. The humid heat transformed the ground into a kaleidoscopic riot of color. Amid a sea of flowers was the grave of the English botanist Joan Margaret Legge, who had a fatal accident while picking flowers and collecting seeds. I had pitched my tent not far from her grave and kept wondering how this solitary botanist had spent her last hours. Was she grateful for being vouchsafed to spend them in this paradise of flowers instead of amid the hubbub of a big city? Himalayan graves tend to induce a mood of melancholy, and one is all too prone to attribute to the deceased the same feeling of ecstasy that one feels oneself in such surroundings. But when the end is near, is the victim still as happy? Is it not even more difficult to take one's leave of the world up here in the mountains than it would be in a dreary hospital ward?

One of the most extraordinary dreamers, or fanatics, who ever pitted his strength against the Himalayas was an Englishman, Captain Maurice Wilson. He made his way to India in a light aircraft, and his original plan was to land as high up on Mount Everest as possible and go on to the summit on foot. The Swiss tried the same idea on Dhaulagiri, but after being suddenly whisked to a height of more than 17,000 feet in their aircraft *Yeti*, they felt like death for a day or two and took a long time to get acclimatized. Wilson was more fortunate: He had the expected difficulties with the authorities over his aircraft and had to leave it in India. Like most other travelers without a permit, he disguised himself as a Tibetan and with only three Sherpas made his way as quickly as possible to the northern slopes of Everest.

The motives of most individualists can be divined with some degree of probability—a love of adventure, the urge to accomplish something sensational, or the desire for self-glorification. But

Wilson seems to have been a more complicated character. Maybe he was a mystic, one for whom the mind is more important than the body. It almost seems as if he had been vouchsafed some visionary perception or other and been imbued with a new faith. Yet how was he to convince mankind of it? Only by an achievement verging on the miraculous: God, who had vouchsafed him the vision, would also work the miracle. Perhaps this explanation is a trifle farfetched, but the more one studies Wilson as a man, the less improbable it seems. The fact remains that God did not work a miracle. After the Sherpas had very sensibly refused to go any farther, Wilson went on alone and got to 21,100 feet before perishing of cold and exhaustion. His body was found by Shipton a year later and buried in eternal snow.

When I saw a film in Hong Kong a year or two ago about how a Red Chinese expedition reached the summit of Mount Everest, I had already heard about Wilson's fate. Since the Chinese reached the summit at night, the film does not include any shots of the moment of triumph, and for me the climax of the film was when the Chinese came upon Wilson's mummified body, freed from its covering of snow by the tremendous wind. Imagine the scene: Fanatical ideologists, straining every nerve to climb the world's highest mountain in order to prove the invincibility of dialectical materialism and the precepts of Mao Tse-tung, were gazing on the features (perfectly preserved in the dry cold) of a man who on the same mountain had been trying to substantiate the teaching of God.

The Chinese expedition to Mount Everest, or such details of it as seeped through to the Western world, is an illustration of collective mountaineering, as favored by the Russians, in an extreme form. No fewer than 300 people of both sexes drove in jeeps from Lhasa to the base camp, although, according to another report, the number was only 214.

In 1961 Shin Chan-chun published a report in the *British Alpine Journal*. Some of its fifty-six paragraphs make astonishing reading, as can be gauged from the following extracts:

1. On 25 May 1960 three young Chinese mountaineers reached the summit of Mt Everest by the difficult northerly route for the first time in the history of mankind.
35. Liu Lien-man was in a state of extreme exhaustion and was stumbling at every step. At 28,700 feet he could go no further.
36. Wang Fu-chou, Chu-Hin-yua and Liu Lien-man, all members of the Communist Party, joined Konbu in a brief Party discussion. It was decided that the assault party should press on to the summit as quickly as possible, and that Liu Lien-man should stay where he was. As their oxygen was used up, they dumped the apparatus...
41. ...and started on the most dangerous and arduous journey in the history of mankind. The summit was reached at 04.20 hours Peking time on 25 May 1960; and a flag, a bust of Mao Tse-tung, and a document giving the names of the party and the date were deposited. It was too dark to take any photographs, but nine geological specimens were collected as a present for Chairman Mao Tse-tung.
52. The success of the Chinese expedition is due to our having adhered to Mao Tse-tung's thoughts on strategy: to disregard difficulties *strategically* but to give them careful consideration *tactically*.

81 Tibetans in ceremonial attire making a pilgrimage to Muktinath in the north of Nepal, where gases escaping from the earth's interior form an "eternal flame." In the background is Mount Dhaulagiri

82 Vasudhara waterfall near Mana (Garhwal). According to a legend, a divinity once rested here and was regaled with nectar

83 and 84 Bridges made of earth, wood, and bamboo. The expectation of life among the Nepalese is only about twenty-six years because there are not enough doctors and too many bridges

85 A Himalayan evening: Manaslu (26,629 feet)

86 A lucky charm outside a Chinese hostelry in south-eastern Tibet

87 Pilgrims resting on the way to Badrinath. Sadhus, among whom well-educated men are often to be found, are accommodated free of charge

88 Chitralis are good mountaineers but lack experience. Even when crossing glaciers, they never wear boots but wrap cloths around their feet and fasten them with straps made of skins

89 A "crawling pilgrim" in Tibet. He will take two months to make his way around Kailas, the sacred mountain, two hours' journey on foot

90, 91 and 92 To negotiate some of the tracks between the vertical walls of the gorges in the main Himalaya range, one must have a head for heights and trust in God

93 Before the road from Katmandu to India was built, it took weeks to drag automobiles to the Nepalese capital, which boasted a mile or two of asphalt streets

54. We succeeded because we were able to profit by the experiences of mountaineers from other countries, particularly from the progressive Soviet Union. Other reasons for our triumph were our firm belief in the victory of the revolution; the collective spirit of solidarity, friendship and brotherhood which our team so conspicuously displayed; their nobility of character; and the Communist precept of putting "side before self."

Compared with the characteristic understatement of British mountaineers (when asked why he wanted to tackle Everest, George Mallory replied, "Because it's there"), the Chinese report is certainly long-winded. In China, art, as well as party doctrine, had a hand in the commemorations of this great success. Shanghai produced a jade carving of Everest and a team of forty-one mountaineers at various stages of their climb, including the scene on the summit. The carving is about five feet long and weighs two and a half tons. The green jade was found in the province of Honan in the same year (1960) that the expedition carried out its mission, and eighteen skilled carvers spent two years and four months on the carving. So for once strict Chinese dogma was adulterated by a measure of romance (and perhaps kitsch)!

Just as the Chinese were determined to prove the superiority of their system in the Himalayas, so about the turn of the century a young Englishman determined to demonstrate the superiority of the white sahib, the master race, "east of Suez." Like so many others before and since, he attempted to reach the forbidden city of Lhasa without stooping to the indignity of a disguise. The "image" he wanted to present was that of an English gentleman, not a suppliant. After countless adventures, hair-raising tests of courage, and excruciating tortures the Tibetans at last prevailed on Henry Savage Landor to recant. His book *Auf verbotenen Wegen in Tibet* ("On Forbidden Ways in Tibet") was a great favorite with our fathers and grandfathers. It went through goodness knows how many editions and was translated into goodness knows how many languages. Even more perhaps than

120

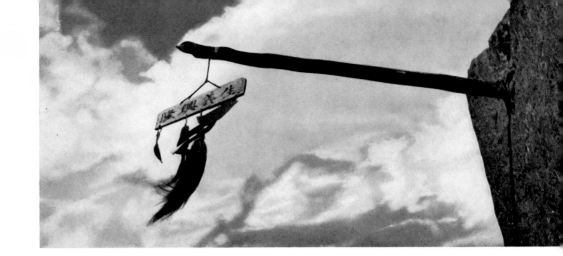

86

87

88

89

90

91

92

93

Sven Hedin's more serious accounts, it kindled Europe's interest in the Himalayas. It is impossible not to sympathize with a stalwart hero who could describe with such composure his own imminent execution: "Nerba, who was holding me by the hair, was told to make me bend my head forward. With the little strength I still had left, and with the desperate courage of a man facing certain death, I resisted, resolved to hold my head high. Of course they could kill me; they could, if they so wished, hack me in pieces, but so long as there was breath in my body these scum were not going to make me bow my head before them. As I stood there, blood pouring from my back, hands and legs, amid an ear-splitting din that was enough to drive one mad, reviled and spat upon by this cowardly mob, I could not have wished for my bitterest enemy to find himself in such a plight. The sword was brandished right up to the side of my neck without quite touching it. And indeed the executioner hesitated to go through with the grisly deed, but the Lamas standing by him gesticulated like madmen and urged him on. With apparent reluctance he repeated the maneuver with the sword against the other side of my neck... It seems that this intimidating swordplay before the actual execution is intended to make the victim's agony even more terrible. It was not until some days later that I learned that on the third repetition of the maneuver the head is really severed."

Apart from his lurid adventures Landor could point to many scientific discoveries and sporting achievements, such as the discovery of the source of the Tsangpo River and of the fact that Manasarowar and Rakas Tal lakes are not connected, not to mention climbing to a height of 22,000 feet. Yet his accounts were regarded as fiction and adventure stories rather than as factual records of actual journeys, and irreverent critics called him an ingenious humbug.

His book appeared in 1898, and the profuse illustrations are reconstructions of sketches and photographs. "The only drawings I did from memory are the torture-scenes, and I trust it will be generally agreed that my impressions are sufficiently vivid." There is also an illustration of the lama monastery of Thokar on Lake Manasarowar. Forty years after Landor's visit I came to the same monastery myself and compared his illustrations with my photographs. How much had changed in the meantime? Had Landor perhaps depicted the mountains as a shade more threatening than they really are? Judge my surprise when I found that his drawings and my photographs were as alike as two peas! Not a wall, not a door, not a window had changed; one could almost pick out the individual stones. It is amazing how these modest buildings have lasted almost half a century without a single repair or modification. But this is not the only part of the Himalayas in which time seems to stand still.

It is also amazing how little methods of travel have changed in the Himalayas. As a young student I once managed to slip into forbidden Tibet disguised as an Indian pilgrim. I was accompanied by two Indians and a Sherpa, and whenever anyone eyed me suspiciously, I pretended to be an idiot. I was very proud of what I thought was entirely my own idea, though I must admit I was a little put out by how readily people accepted my deception. Of course, the important thing was to avoid being recognized. Since then, I have read accounts of a good many journeys to Tibet both before and after my own, and in practically every case the intruder relates how he was obliged to pretend to be an idiot to cover his inadequate knowledge of the language and local habits. And in every case the author seems to be quite sure that the stratagem was a completely original idea.

A man being beheaded. (From Henry S. Landor, *Auf verbotenen Wegen in Tibet*, Leipzig, 1898)

One of the most remarkable attributes of the Swedish explorer Sven Hedin was his amazing memory. In 1936 I wrote a book about my journey to Tibet and asked Hedin, who was the first to explore this particular part of the world, to contribute a foreword. Unfortunately there was a geographical slip in the manuscript I sent him: I had put an island in Rakas Tal Lake instead of in Manasarowar Lake. Somewhat ruffled, Hedin asked me whether I was questioning his geographical accuracy. I admitted my mistake, the misunderstanding was cleared up, and Hedin wrote a charming introduction.

Then came the Second World War, and I heard no more of him. It was not until 1952 that I found myself in Stockholm again. I rang him up and asked whether I might come and see him. At the time he was being visited by Germans, and he obviously didn't recognize my nome, but he invited me to come and see him in the afternoon. When I came into the room, he was signing autographs for a group of visitors. Eventually he turned to me. "What can I do for you?" he asked. I produced my visiting card. Without a second's hesitation he patted me on the shoulder and said with a laugh: "Well, old friend, have you decided where that island is yet, in Manasarowar or Rakas Tal?" It had been sixteen years since the original episode, and in that time he must have written dozens of introductions to books by his imitators.

Another example of Hedin's prodigious memory was given me by Torgny Oberg, who had been brought up by Swedish missionaries in a Mongolian village. Hedin arrived at this village on one of his first large-scale expeditions, and naturally his visit was a red-letter day in the lives of his compatriots the missionaries. Torgny was only a child at the time, but his mother never got tired of telling him what Swedish specialties she had regaled the celebrated explorer with. About fifty years later Torgny returned to Sweden and, like me, called on the by now aging Hedin.

"You won't remember," began Torgny, "but many years ago you visited my parents in Mongolia, Oberg was their name—" "Yes, yes," Hedin interrupted him, "and your mother was very kind to me. She gave me…" and he proceeded to reel off all the dishes that Torgny had so often heard his mother reciting.

Amid the Crossfire of World Politics

"Where the spheres of interest of the great powers intersect, you will usually find a string of small buffer states that manage to maintain a measure of independence." Nowhere is the truth of this dictum brought home more forcibly than in the Himalayas. The string of more or less independent states between India and Tibet stretches from Ladakh, in the arid northwest, and Kashmir, Nepal, Sikkim, and Bhutan to the rain-drenched NEFA. Wooed or threatened by both sides, they yet contrive to maintain their independence. Geographical rigors—the world's highest mountains and the world's most arduous passes—might seem to form a natural frontier precluding any form of aggressive policy. Yet even before Chinese machine guns were turned on India from the Himalayas, the high mountains were no longer an obstacle to the political moves of the two antagonists. Only the players were not the same: Russia's place was taken by China and Britain's by India. But the moves were the same.

When Britain established a Sikkim protectorate in the nineteenth century, China was weak and, despite protests from Lhasa, had to put a good face on a *fait accompli*. Fearing further British penetration, the thirteenth Dalai Lama sent a Mongolian lama to St. Petersburg to ask the czar for assistance. Although in all probability only vague promises were forthcoming, this move prompted Britain to send a military mission under Colonel Francis Younghusband to Lhasa, thus "opening up" Tibet from the south.

Now that Britain has delegated her rights and responsibilities to India, and China is firmly established in Tibet and Sinkiang, the situation is quite different, and the main pressure is southward. While the Chinese thrust down through the NEFA (though the invaders soon withdrew) was keeping India and the world at large on tenterhooks, events in Ladakh passed almost unnoticed. In 1956–57 the Chinese built a road from Sinkiang to Gartok in Tibet. About 110 miles of it ran through the Indian territory of Aksai Chin, an uninhabited plateau that is extremely cold in winter. Incredible as it may seem, it was not until a year later that the Indians heard about this motor road, on which no fewer than 3,000 workmen had been employed. There were one or two skirmishes, and diplomatic notes were sent to Peking referring to "minor frontier incidents." In the end the Chinese retained possession of their vitally important road and claimed 15,000 square miles of this no-man's-land.

Since the partition of the Indian subcontinent, Kashmir and its capital Srinagar, which used to be a tourist paradise, a sort of "Venice above the clouds," have been to all intents and purposes in a state of war. United Nations delegations have come and gone, without achieving anything except maintaining an armed truce between India and Pakistan. A Delhi newspaper complained that "there was a time when the Himalayan passes were the gateways to the holy places of Tibet: now they are the gateways to the fertile plains of India."

The lama monastery of Thokar on Manasarowar Lake. (From Henry S. Landor, *Auf verbotenen Wegen in Tibet*)

In 1948 some of Gandhi's ashes were strewn over the sacred lake of Manasarowar, but "nowadays Hindus no longer dare to cast the ashes of their loved ones into the sacred lake, for fear the sons of China should regard them as nuclear powder," opined an Indian writer, who went on to quote from the Bhagavad-Gita: "If thou failest to fight this just fight, thou shalt not have lived according to the law, and thine honor shall be besmirched." Nepal, Sikkim, and Bhutan show little inclination to "fight this just fight" or even to endorse it. Perhaps they realize, from bitter experience, that it is wiser for small countries not to provoke their powerful neighbors. They may also hold the view that China is more powerful than India, in which case it would be less injudicious to provoke Delhi than to annoy Peking.

In order to demonstrate the country's independence, Nepal time is ten minutes ahead of India's. And it was in defiance of India's displeasure that King Mahendra accepted a Chinese offer to build a "road of friendship" from the Tibetan frontier to Katmandu. Today food supplies are carried by trucks from adjacent Nepal to the Chinese troops in Tibet, and political propaganda is carried by the same route, only in the opposite direction. The king's comment is said to have been: "Do you really imagine Communism is imported in taxis?"

In Tibet the Chinese have built a network of roads taking in seventeen different passes leading to Nepal. While Chinese troops are stationed right on the frontier, Nepalese troops are not to be posted within 12 miles of it. China has refused to withdraw her troops because to do so would

132

An old Tibetan map

encourage patriotic Tibetan guerrilla activities. During Hillary's yeti expedition his walkie-talkies were completely jammed by the "China-wallahs," as the Sherpas called them, broadcasting Chinese operas on the same wavelength.

Yet like other great powers, China is providing Nepal with development aid, particularly to industries that will make Nepal independent of India. The perpetual tug-of-war for the Himalayan countries still goes on, and since the 1950's, when Indian influence was predominant, Nepal has managed to preserve a proud, though precarious, independence. It has to keep its feet firmly on the narrow path between two mutually hostile neighbors. Economically Nepal is dependent on India, militarily on China.

So far there have been no serious difficulties between Nepal and China. Maybe better roads, air connections, and radio service have stimulated Nepalese nationalism, and even Sherpas and other peoples of Tibetan origin probably regard themselves nowadays as Nepalese.

A good illustration of this trend is the "King of Mustang." His country, just north of Annapurna, is a sort of wedge driven up northward into the Tibetan plateau. He is quite independent of Katmandu, and the scenery and way of life are more Tibetan than Nepalese. When I called on him in his castle and asked to take some photographs, he politely refused; it was Friday, and surely I knew that Friday was an unlucky day? I had forgotten about this superstition, which is particularly popular in Katmandu. I remember once some people who had booked a flight to India for a Friday leaving their home the day before and staying the night with friends, which meant that the journey had been started on Thursday.

The royal dynasty of Mustang goes back to the eighteenth century. During the troubles between Tibet and the Gurkhas the son of a Gurkha raja was posted to this inaccessible plateau. In due course he set up a kingdom of his own and married a Tibetan girl. His heirs also went to Tibet for their wives and adopted the Tibetan way of life. Today, Mustang is just like any other small Tibetan town. Nevertheless, the king is proud of his Nepalese origin. He is a general in the Nepalese army, and his son is a colonel. He stresses his kinship with King Mahendra and manages to preserve an astute diplomatic equilibrium along this tricky frontier: wives from Tibet, allegiance to Katmandu.

The only incident that disturbed relations between Nepal and China was a "cartological discrepancy." Nepal's pride and joy is Mount Everest, and there was great indignation in Katmandu when it was announced that China was claiming its southern slopes. Despite a Chinese denial the Prime Minister of Nepal ventured to assert that the entire summit was Nepalese territory; only the northern slopes belonged to Tibet. The summit was the property of the country "down to which it slopes." The Chinese, who in the meantime had climbed Mount Everest from the north, refused to accept this formula. Eventually the question of the summit was left amid the clouds that usually cover it. On the map issued after the 1961 agreement the frontier is marked as passing exactly through the center of the summit.

Vagueness about the exact delineation of the frontier goes back to the 1904 Conference at Simla, at which representatives of Britain, China, and Tibet met under the chairmanship of Sir Arthur McMahon to agree on a political frontier through virtually unexplored mountain country. After protracted discussions McMahon casually picked up a bit of chalk and drew lines from one mighty

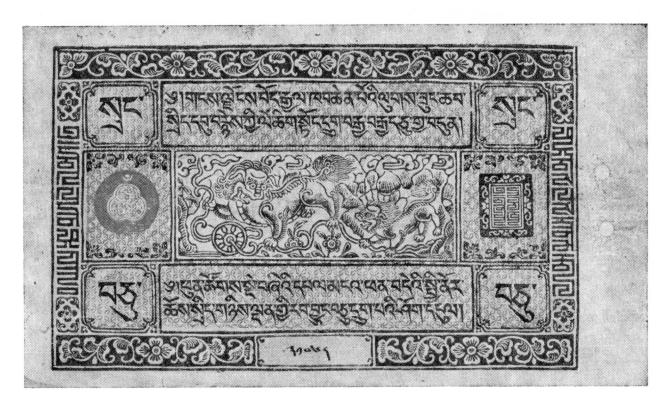

A Tibetan banknote (actual size)

A silver Nepalese rupee, mid-nineteenth century (actual size)

Nepalese rupee and half rupee, mid-twentieth century (actual sizes)

peak to the next. This zigzag line, the oft-quoted McMahon Line, was to be the frontier. China never recognized it, and up in the mountains it was never marked, presumably because nobody, except possibly a yeti, would have been able to trace it.

As well as geographical and frontier problems there have been historical and political difficulties. All the Himalayan countries have always been to a greater or lesser extent dependent on China. It is for historical reasons that China refuses to recognize Indian rights in Sikkim, Bhutan, and parts of the NEFA and insists on conducting bilateral negotiations with these countries individually. Chinese maps show 300 square miles of eastern Bhutan as part of Tibet, yet an Indian map gives the whole of Bhutan as an Indian province. The difference of opinion over Mount Everest has in this case swollen to out-and-out "cartological warfare," at Bhutan's expense.

Delhi's tone of voice is often wounding to Himalayan pride. Whereas the British always wanted a neutral Tibet as India's northern bastion, Delhi has lately come to regard the Himalayas as India's northern ramparts and seems to forget that in some districts the actual frontier runs a long way to the south. Nehru, for instance, announced that "from time immemorial the Himalayas have been our superb frontier. Today of course they are not as insurmountable as they were, but they still constitute a formidable barrier... Whenever India's security is threatened we look upon the Himalayas as our frontier. We recognize the independence of Nepal and we wish her well, but any child knows that the only way to get to Nepal is through India."

America is showing more and more interest in Nepal, and this is to Nepal's advantage insofar as if Russia offered substantial development aid, the United States would refuse to be outdone, and vice versa. But when there were alleged to have been discussions in Delhi about a plan to divide Nepal into an American sphere of influence in the north and an Indian equivalent in the south, Katmandu felt obliged to decline the well-meaning solicitude of both suitors.

The King of Bhutan also maintained an attitude of the utmost reserve during the frontier incidents between India and China and declined Indian offers of assistance on the grounds that the incidents were due to misunderstandings that could best be cleared up on the spot. Peking, of course, may well have placed an entirely different interpretation on them. As the "Middle of the World," Old China divided countries not under her direct rule into neighboring territories under local governments approved by the emperor, *t'u-ssu*, and foreign countries, *wei-kuo*. Although China has broken with her past, she is by no means averse to bringing up historical facts that could, if manipulated, lead to claims. Bhutan was definitely a *t'u-ssu*.

By means of comprehensive reforms the King of Bhutan is doing all he can to consolidate the stability of his country without becoming dependent on his two mighty neighbors. Forty thousand refugees from Tibet were given decent political asylum; 5,000 Indians who had been abducted to Bhutan as slaves were set free; and 175,000 Nepalese immigrants, long regarded as second-class citizens, have been granted full civil rights.

Strategically, Bhutan is the most important of all the Himalayan countries. Only 60 miles of Indian territory separate Bhutan from East Pakistan, and a Chinese invasion would immediately cut India off from the rich territory of Assam. The capital of Bhutan is only 120 miles from Lhasa and 180 miles from storm-tossed Burma.

136

94 Trade route in central Nepal

But it is not strategic factors, and it is not modern weapons that have made the Himalayas such a dangerous frontier. The dispute over the world's highest mountain is more likely to be conducted in terms of conflicting ideologies than by a recourse to arms. Two totally different political systems, two totally different ways of life are in immediate proximity, and subversive agitators will find a way over even the most elaborately defended pass.

Delhi no doubt harbors nostalgic memories of Chou En-lai's state visit, when crowds, hundreds of thousands strong, chanted, "*Hindi-Chindi-bhai-bhai*" ("Indians and Chinese are brothers"). Today they are enemies, and the Himalayas are no longer the insurmountable barrier that they used to be.

Himalayan Conquerors

In his *Erschliessung des Himalaya (The Exploration of the Himalayas)*, published in 1933, Michael Kurz called Mount Everest the "globe's third pole." That great Himalayan expert Günter Dyhrenfurth chose this apt phrase as the title of his widely read book, which is informed by an accuracy and comprehensiveness that have made it the bible of the Himalayas. Today, the "third pole" is universally accepted as referring to the Himalayas and the Karakorum.

Psychologically, there could be no more appropriate name for high mountains. Like the North and South Poles, peaks of 25,000 feet and higher have no intrinsic value or scientific significance. Amid a monotonous expanse of ice, his compass and his calculations will tell the polar explorer that he has reached the end of his agonizing trek and can hoist a flag and make for home as one of the immortals in the history of exploration. But the "third pole" is a more distinct and a more dramatic goal. There is probably no enterprise in the world that offers so much effort and so much glamor as the conquest of a mountain. It has all the requisites: walls of rock, wind, avalanches, icy cold, failure and death. Keep going, and you get to the top. Nothing more to climb; you can't go any higher; you've made it. In no other activity can the difference between success and disaster be more brutally clear-cut.

Early travelers in the Himalayas—Chinese pilgrims, Christian missionaries, Indian pundits—regarded mountains either as obstacles in their path or as geographical features to be identified or recorded on maps. They were followed by explorers who, although their objectives were primarily scientific or political, made a close study of the mountains they encountered and occasionally ventured to pit their strength against them, but with little success until mountaineering had been taken up and developed in the European Alps. It is impossible to give a complete list of all the men who did such valuable pioneer work in the Himalayas and Karakorum. A few names must suffice. There was for instance the veterinary surgeon William Moorcroft, who traveled all over the Pamirs, Karakorum, Hindu Kush, and Tibet and died in Afghanistan in 1825. A few years ago one could still see his name where he had scratched it on a wall in the Buddhist caves of Bamian. There used to be a story that his "death" was only a ruse and that in reality he went to Lhasa in disguise and lived on there for another ten years without being spotted.

Sir Joseph Dalton Hooker, who explored Sikkim in 1848, was a great Kanchenjunga enthusiast. His *Himalayan Journals* is still a standard work and widely read. Then there were W. M. Conway, who led a Karakorum expedition; the Duke of Abruzzi; Sven Hedin; the W. H. Workmans (husband and wife); Philip C. Visser; and the photographer Vittorio Sella, who about the turn of the century took some photographs that are still unsurpassed.

The first "mountaineer," in the strict sense of the word, to lock horns with the Himalayas was the Englishman W. W. Graham, who arrived in 1883 "to enjoy some sport and adventure, not to expand the frontiers of human knowledge." With the help of some Swiss guides he claimed to have climbed Kabru (24,215 feet), but there is an element of doubt about whether he actually did, since he was often not sure where he really was.

Graham was not, however, the first mountaineer with Alpine experience to tackle a peak of 20,000 feet. The pioneers in this respect were three brothers from Munich; Adolf, Hermann, and Robert von Schlagintweit. In Switzerland they had climbed Monte Rosa without guides, but it was on a natural history expedition to Central Asia from 1854 to 1858 that they first came under the spell of high mountains. On Abi Gamin they got to a height of 22,500 feet, which in those days and with their limited experience and primitive equipment was a magnificent performance, and it was not until ninety-five years later that a Swiss expedition was the first to reach the summit of Abi Gamin. The Schlagintweit brothers possessed an insatiable thirst for knowledge and an unconquerable spirit of enterprise, and they might well have become the first to conquer a peak of 20,000 feet or more had not Adolf been murdered in Kashgar.

Meantime, the Survey of India had measured the heights of all the Himalayan peaks, and there was actually a story of an unnamed Indian assistant having lugged a theodolite up the 23,000-foot Shilla. It sounds incredible: While the white sahibs hire expert mountaineers from Switzerland and spend fortunes on their expeditions, a young Indian, practically barefoot and earning only a few rupees a month, makes light of a climb of 23,000 feet and gets on with his work, unhonored and unsung, without the slightest inkling of the magnitude of his achievement! In point of fact the story cannot be true, because in the Punjab Himalayas there is no peak higher than 21,400 feet. The first peak of 23,000 feet or over to be climbed was Trisul, 23,500 feet, in 1907.

Another story in connection with the Survey of India goes back to 1852, when a young employee came bursting into the director's office and stammered: "Sir, I've just discovered the world's highest mountain!" As Peak XV it was measured from six different points more than 60 miles apart, and the result was 29,028 feet, which in fact did make it the highest peak in the survey's records. The British had no name for it, and Hermann von Schlagintweit, who had visited Nepal, maintained that it must be Gauri Sankar, which in reality is about 35 miles from Everest and "only" 25,478 feet high. The Tibetans call the world's highest mountain Chomolungma (literally, "Goddess Mother of the Land"), while to Indians and Nepalese it is Sagarmatha, the "Summit of Heaven." Eventually it was named Everest in honor of Sir George Everest, who for many years was the head of the Survey of India, and its name is hardly likely to be changed. So it was relatively recently in the world's history that its highest mountain was identified. In the eighteenth century Titlis, Mont Blanc, and finally Chimborazo in South America were thought to be the highest. As the Himalayas

95 Camp 3 of the 1965 German Himalayan expedition. In the background is the "Nepalese Matterhorn," Machapuchare (20,990 feet)

96 and **97** The progress of an ice avalanche on the south side of the main Batura range in the northwestern Karakorum. The avalanche started from a height of more than 6,600 feet

98 A cross for a member of the Austrian Dhaulagiri expedition who lost his life

99 An avalanche in the Batura fills the valley with particles of snow for miles around. The cross is a memorial to three British and two German mountaineers who perished here in 1959, presumably in one of these tremendous avalanches. Their bodies were never found

100 Hermann Buhl on his second 25,000-foot conquest, Broad Peak (26,397 feet), in the Karakorum. A few days later Buhl had a fatal accident

were gradually explored, the honor passed successively to Dhaulagiri, Kanchenjunga, and Everest.

The exploration of the Himalayas really got under way at the start of the present century, and the record height of 22,500 feet reached by the Schlagintweit brothers was perpetually being broken, the stages being Pyramid Peak (23,430 feet); Bride Peak (25,160 feet) by the Duke of Abruzzi's 1909 expedition; 27,300 feet on Everest in 1922; and two years later 27,850 feet on the same mountain. But although heights of more than 26,500 feet had been reached, none of the peaks of 26,000 feet or more had been climbed.

After the Second World War the race was resumed in earnest, sporting ambition and national prestige being the main incentives. Friendly diplomatic relations were an important and sometimes decisive factor, because many of the highest peaks were in countries that could not be entered without permits. A principle was soon established whereby an expedition applied for an official permit from the country in which its objective was situated. This was a good idea because it obviated the danger of there being more porters (who live off the land) than the somewhat barren valleys could provide food for. License fees were introduced, irrespective of success or failure. From now on, permits for an assault on one of Nepal's 26,000-footers were going to cost money.

For many mountains there was a queue: the French, say, in the spring; in the autumn the British; in the following spring the Swiss. But one expedition after another came to grief, more than fifty in fact, before the first 26,000-footer, Annapurna, was conquered. Mount Everest alone repulsed eleven expeditions, British and Swiss, before it fell to Hillary and Tensing. On Nanga Parbat, the "killer mountain," eight expeditions had to capitulate with considerable loss of life before Buhl got to the top alone. It began to look as if there must be some truth in the superstition that the high mountains were the abode of the gods and no mortal being could ever hope to violate them. It was not until 1950 that the spell was broken by the French conquest of Annapurna, and within the ensuing ten years all the remaining 26,000-footers were climbed except Shisha Pangma, which held out until 1964 because it was in Tibet and therefore off limits to Western expeditions. The plans and preparations of half a century eventually came to fruition in an extraordinarily short space of time.

There is a rational explanation of this. Developments in the technique of climbing and the quality of the equipment were rapid and far-reaching. The new materials afforded infinitely better protection against cold and severe weather. Artificial oxygen (what the Sherpas call "British air") obviates

96

97

98

99

the risk of shortage of breath or losing consciousness at high altitudes. Better cookers, food in concentrated form, and new medicines stimulated the body's resistance to sudden collapse, while familiarity with the local climate and the availability of radio weather forecasts minimized the danger of being taken by surprise by the monsoon. In my view the psychological factor was also important. The spell of the invincibility of the 26,000-footers was broken. Their summits were no longer a wildly irrational dream but a practical possibility.

There have been books by the members of nearly every successful—and unsuccessful—assault on a 26,000-footer, with a mass of detailed information and vivid description. This is not, therefore, the place for more than a brief description of some of the outstanding milestones in the conquest of the Himalayas, starting with the following list of peaks of 26,000 feet or over, their height, the date of their first conquest, and the nationality of the expedition concerned.

	Height (Feet)	Date of First Climb	Nationality
Everest	29,028	1953	British
K2	28,250	1954	Italian
Kanchenjunga	28,216	1955	British
Lhotse	27,890	1956	Swiss
Makalu	27,824	1955	French
Dhaulagiri	26,795	1960	Swiss (Diemberger)
Cho Oyu	26,680 (?)	1954	Austrian
Nanga Parbat	26,629	1953	German (Buhl)
Manaslu	26,629	1956	Japanese
Annapurna	26,502	1950	French
Hidden Peak	26,467	1958	American
Broad Peak	26,397	1957	Austrian
Gasherbrum II	26,352	1956	Austrian
Shisha Pangma	26,285	1964	Chinese

Three or four of these climbs aroused worldwide enthusiasm, and one or two others attracted widespread favorable comment; but one had to be very well informed indeed to know whether Shisha Pangma had really been climbed or not.

The first 26,000-footer to surrender was Annapurna, conquered in a brilliant exploit by a French expedition under Maurice Herzog. His very severe frostbite and his account, *Annapurna, The First 26,000 Footer*, written with characteristic Gallic humor, aroused worldwide admiration and sympathy.

As the world's highest mountain, Mount Everest had always been the ultimate aspiration, and the number of expeditions that came to grief on its slopes only whetted Himalayan appetites. The announcement of Hillary's triumph on the very day of Queen Elizabeth II's coronation in London was certainly a brilliant piece of stage management. For some strange reason there were one or

two fanatics in India who put out a lot of nonsense in an attempt to prove that the summit had never been reached. What made this attitude all the more difficult to comprehend was that the success of Sherpa Tensing, who travels on an Indian passport, made him a national hero all over Asia.

Nanga Parbat became known as the "German graveyard" because of the high casualties it inflicted on German expeditions. The great British mountaineer A. F. Mummery also perished on it. When it was at last conquered, it must have seemed to German mountaineers like the end of an interminable nightmare. Hermann Buhl's magnificent solo effort was against the wishes of the leader of the expedition, Karl Herligkoffer. His bivouac at 26,400 feet without proper protection from the cold, where he spent the night standing up because the slope was too steep to lie down on, excited the admiration of the entire world. He reached the summit on his own, the only proof of his achievement being a photograph taken from it. Although nobody seriously doubted that he really had reached the top, the photograph was handed over to a scientific institute for a thorough scrutiny: Did the length of the shadows and optical details confirm Buhl's claim? As a Swiss mountaineer observed: "What a world, when a gentleman's word is subjected to scientific confirmation!"

If the conquest of Nanga Parbat was a stupendous solo effort, that of K2 was a triumph of superb organization and a lavish array of equipment and manpower. K2, apart from being a magnificent mountain, is the second highest peak in the world. It was given the designation K2 during the survey of the Karakorum and has been known as K2 ever since, although the locals call it Chogori and the British suggested it should be called after the man who was the first to explore this territory, Henry Haversham Godwin-Austen. Since the Duke of Abruzzi had led a K2 expedition in 1909, the Italians felt they had priority rights to this mountain, and since by this time 26,000-footers were going down like ninepins, they were determined to preclude any possibility of failure. The result was 35,000 pounds of equipment, a party of 30 Italian mountaineers and scientists, and 600 porters.

"I lost my foothold and balance and began to slide down the slope at a terrifying speed, accompanied on my involuntary descent by masses of ice and snow, and by the horrified cries of my coolies. I immediately perceived the danger of being swept into the torrent and from there into the long tunnel of ice in which death was certain. But in those fleeting seconds I had time to wonder whether the stones in the water would check my fall or whether my impetus would deposit me head over heels in the water. I tried to cling on to the hard snow with my frozen fingers and to dig my heels in, but to no purpose. Suddenly I saw in front of me a large rock sticking up out of the snow. It was my last hope, and by desperately straining every muscle and every nerve I endeavoured to divert the direction of my fall to within range of it, cautiously sticking out my legs to take the force of the impact. The shock was terrific and I felt as if every bone in my body were broken. But it arrested my headlong descent, and I was saved—only a foot or two from the torrent's edge." (From Henry S. Landor, *Auf verbotenen Wegen in Tibet*)

The two who conducted the final successful assault on the summit were Lino Lacedelli and Achiele Compagnoni.

The outstanding feature of the Austrian expeditions that had three first conquests to their credit was the Spartan austerity of their equipment, which was not always "according to plan" but was dictated by this small country's limited financial resources. The Cho Oyu expedition consisted of only three Austrians, and the baggage weighed only 1,800 pounds. It was the smallest expedition that ever tackled a 26,000-footer. On Broad Peak the four Austrian sahibs acted as their own porters.

101 Dhaulagiri, the "white mountain" (26,795 feet)
102 A conglomeration of granite and slate on the 3,500-foot west wall of Torichmir West IV (24,115 feet)
103 Mount Everest (29,028 feet), the world's highest mountain; an unusual view from the north
104 and 105 Siniolchu (22,625 feet) in the Sikkim Himalayas, often called "the world's most beautiful mountain." These photographs were taken by the Italian Vittorio Sella in 1909
106 The grave of Alfred Drexel, a victim of the "killer mountain," Nanga Parbat
107 The fairy-tale fields at the foot of Nanga Parbat which the German Nanga Parbat expedition chose for its main camp
108 and 109 An expedition resting in the woods and entering the glacier zone
110 Morning by the Baltoro Glacier. In the center is the peak of Muztagh (23,900 feet)
111 Ski sticks are often very useful at great heights and in deep snow
112 Porters on the 1954 Italian expedition's successful assault on K2 (28,250 feet) in the Karakorum
113 and 114 The start—and sometimes the end—of an expedition. Artificial oxygen and the latest products of the food and textile industries are mobilized, but severe weather can make nonsense of the most carefully laid plans
115 A "stone-man" built by mountaineers in the Annapurna group; in the background, right, the still unclimbed Patal-Hiunchuli (20,920 feet)
116 The German Nanga Parbat expedition's Camp 2 at 17,820 feet

117 Porters making their way to the above camp after a heavy fall of snow
118 A steep arête (at about 21,200 feet) on the northwest shoulder of Siniolchu (22,725 feet)
119 Negotiating ice on Nanga Parbat
120 An ice crevasse on Nanga Parbat
121 This member of the Italian K2 expedition looks like someone from Mars
122 Hermann Buhl, who got to the top of Nanga Parbat alone, after his second big conquest, Broad Peak (26,397 feet)
123 Two members of the German Nanga Parbat ski expedition, Aloys Thurmayr and Georg Huber, died of exhaustion at Camp 4 (23,660 feet) in the spring of 1964
124 Herbert Tichy after the first conquest of Cho Oyu. His hands were so badly frostbitten that he even had to have help to enjoy a smoke
125 The "collective" conquest of Shisha Pangma (26,285 feet) by a joint Chinese-Tibetan expedition in 1964. This was the last 26,000-footer to be climbed. It is in Tibet, and the Chinese mobilized a lavish array of men and equipment
126 A view of Tibet and a sea of 20,000-footers from the summit of Broad Peak (26,397 feet)
127 Lino Lacedelli, a member of the successful Italian expedition, on the summit of K2, the second highest mountain in the world
128 Maurice Herzog being carried down Annapurna by Sherpas. He had severe frostbite after the first conquest of the mountain
129 Celebration: after the successful assault on Cho Oyu, Sepp Jöchler had to drink an awful lot of chang

After two unsuccessful attempts on Manaslu, the Japanese met with a distinctly hostile reception from the normally friendly inhabitants of the town of Sama. Volleys of stones, yaks' excrement, and abuse forced this massive expedition—13 Japanese, 14 tons of equipment, and 450 porters—to return to Katmandu. The people of Sama were convinced that the earlier abortive attempts on Manaslu had provoked the wrath of the gods and were responsible for avalanches, drought, and the pox. Two years later, in 1956, the Japanese were back again. This time the people of Sama were much more helpful and allowed the expedition to proceed on its way unmolested. Like the good diplomats they are, the Japanese had taken the precaution of sending on in advance gifts of sewing machines, which excited so much curiosity that the wrath of the Manaslu gods was quite forgotten.

About the successful expeditions one could write either volumes or just a few lines. Most of them followed the same old familiar pattern: difficulties with porters, progress, setbacks, maybe

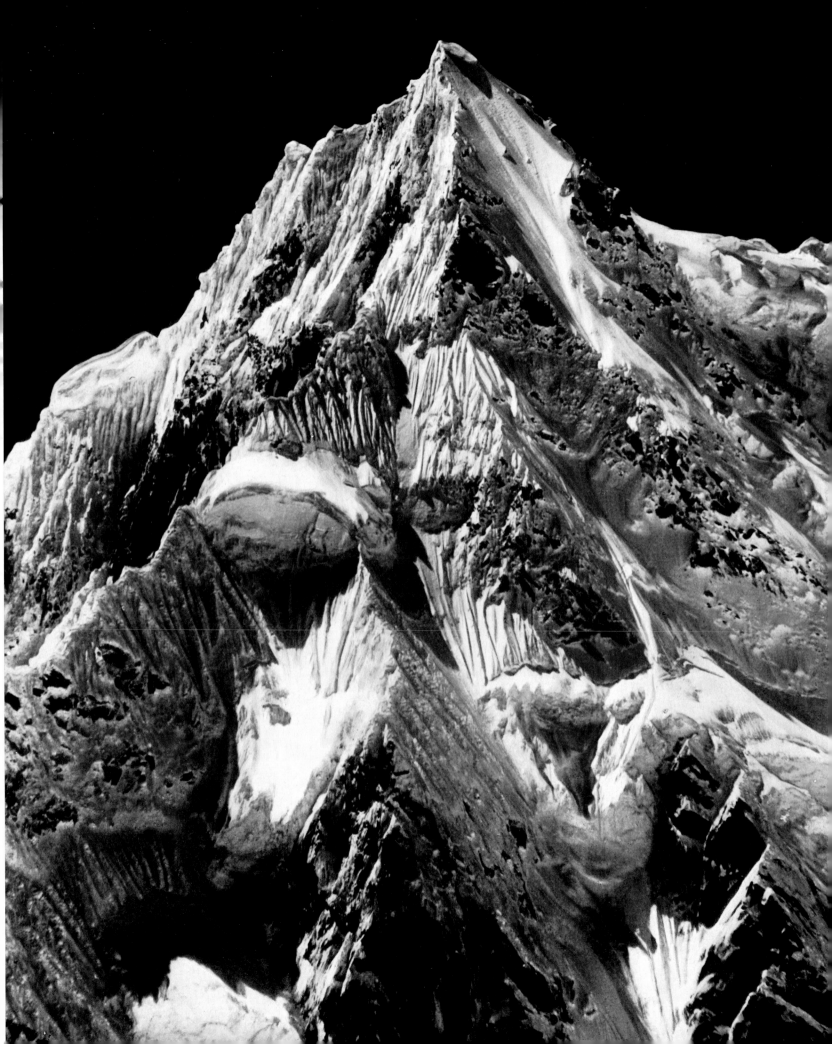

106

107

108

109   110

111

112

113

114

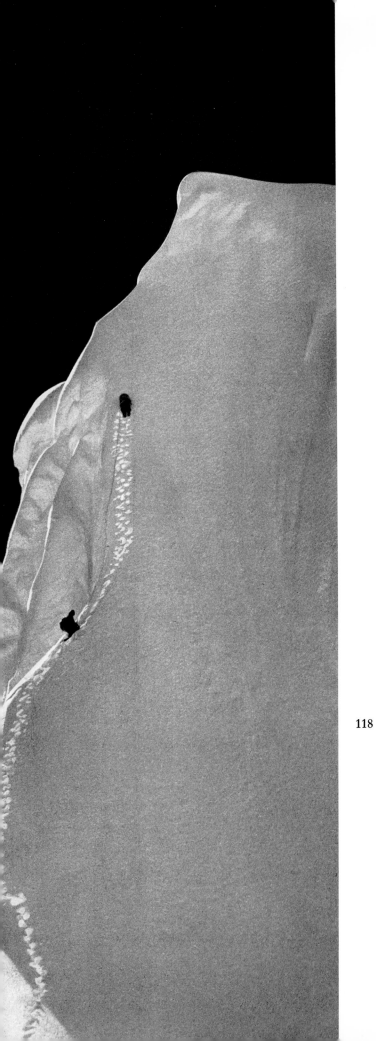

118   119

121

122

123

124

125

126

127

128

a disaster, a victim who never lived to tell his friends back home how superb the Himalayas are, and finally the summit, the crowning success. "Like happy and fortunate nations, successful expeditions have no history," wrote Jean Franco of the French Makalu expedition. Every single member of it got to the top, sat around as if they were in the Alps in warm sunshine, and were only sorry the mountain wasn't a thousand feet or so higher (an unusual wish on a 26,000-footer)!

It may perhaps seem surprising to find two Asian nations—Japan and China—on the roll of honor. The Chinese, who in olden times would rather enjoy a mountain in a painting than have to climb one, learned a great deal from their Russian teachers. However dubious their alleged conquest of Everest may be, their successes on Shisha Pangma and other mountains are sufficient proof that their equipment, technique, and experience have made them worthy Himalayan challengers. As for the Japanese, the centuries'-old Fujiyama pilgrimage has taught them to bring the same concentration and characteristic tenacity to mountaineering that they have to skiing. They also seem to have access to more generous funds than some other countries. In recent years there have sometimes been several Japanese expeditions in the Himalayas at the same time.

Another factor has been the emancipation of Asian women. In 1961 a Chinese women's expedition tackled Kongur I (25,010 feet), and two members of it (Tibetans actually) reached the summit, which may make them challengers for the "women's altitude record" set up by the Frenchwoman Claude Kogan, who climbed to about 25,700 feet on Cho Oyu in 1954. Subsequently, she lost her life in an avalanche on this same mountain, along with the Belgian woman Claudine van der Stratten and two Sherpas, when leading a similar all-women expedition.

It is to the Chinese that we owe the debunking of the legend of Amne Machin. During World War II an American pilot flying over the "hump" between India and China suddenly found himself confronted by a peak that he estimated must be about 29,500 feet high. In 1948 the Americans made some reconnaissance flights and a year later made an overhasty attempt to survey the mountain with lamentably primitive instruments. They calculated that it must indeed be about 29,500 feet high. Mountaineers were beginning to indulge in dreams of a super Everest, until in 1960 an expedition launched by the Peking Geological Institute climbed the mountain and found that it was a mere 23,520 feet.

I cannot say that my personal memories of Amne Machin, the "father of the peacock," are particularly happy. I have never actually seen it, but I once made a fruitless journey of about 250 miles in the hope of doing so. The reason why Amne Machin is so difficult to get at is that the Ngoloks who live at its foot are an exceedingly pugnacious tribe. On my way from China I ran into an American missionary in Labrang, in Tibet. He was on friendly terms with the Ngoloks and had learned their language. Some of them had come to Labrang to do some business and pray at the local monastery, and they wanted to take the American back with them. He in turn was willing to take me along at my own expense. Unfortunately I had left all my money at Lanchow, about 120 miles away. Time was short, so I shot off to Lanchow, reached it in two and a half days, and returned to Labrang at the same breakneck speed with bags of silver yuans. The missionary was still there; the Chinese had intervened with a veto, and all I had to show for my attempt to get to Amne Machin was blistered feet and the nickname *Pi ma k'uai tien erh*—"Faster than a horse."

Lake with the sacred Mount Kailas. (From Henry S. Landon, *Auf verbotenen Wegen in Tibet*)

As soon as present political obstacles are disposed of, proceedings in the Himalayas will follow the familiar Alpine pattern: first conquest, second and subsequent conquests, a new route, a crossing, more rapid conquests, winter climb, climb on skis, a women's expedition, and so on. This is no fanciful dream. Everest, Nanga Parbat, and Cho Oyu have already been climbed more than once. Americans have crossed Everest via the hitherto untrodden west shoulder, over the summit, and down to the south saddle. On a controversial conquest of Cho Oyu on skis (controversial because the photographs allegedly taken from the summit are not particularly convincing), two Germans, Aloys Thurmayr and Georg Huber, perished of exhaustion.

Mountaineers in the Himalayas will have to contend with exactly the same difficulties as in the Alps, except that the approach routes are far longer, everything is on an infinitely vaster scale, temperatures are murderously low, and the weather can be lethal. Not to mention the problem of the "Zone of Death." Which is not, as one might at first suppose, a figment of a journalist thirsting for a scoop, but an expression coined by the Swiss doctor Edouard Wyss-Dunant. In 1953 he wrote: "One can acclimatize oneself to heights of about 20,000 feet but not to 23,000 feet, when the time available for adaptation is strictly limited owing to one's loss of energy not being made up during rest or sleep. Maybe it will be possible one day to raise the acclimatization height a bit, but not very much."

Probably the doctor was being unduly pessimistic, because lack of oxygen affects different people in different ways. There are several instances of climbs up to 26,200 feet without oxygen apparatus and of considerable exertions without unpleasant consequences. Up to about 49,000 feet the composition of the atmosphere is proportionately the same: 21 percent oxygen and 78 percent nitrogen.

170

Lack of oxygen is a result of a drop in atmospheric pressure and the expansion of the gases. But all these scientific data are not much help when in a tent at 23,000 feet one cannot even get one's boots on without falling back exhausted every few seconds in order to get one's breath. This is an ordeal that personally, thank God, I have never had to endure in the so-called Zone of Death about 25,500 feet, but I can imagine it must be fearful. Every step forward left one gasping for breath. I was told later in Hong Kong that we had been treating ourselves to a typically capitalist luxury. The film of the Red Chinese expedition to Everest was being shown at at a Red Chinese club. Afterward there was a friendly exchange of experiences, in the course of which I was asked how many times I needed to draw breath to take a single step at 25,500 feet. The Chinese comrades said they had managed with four on Everest. I had to confess that we needed more like twenty breaths before lifting a foot off the ground, but that this of course, was one of the disadvantages of the capitalist system. Laughter and friendliness all round. Even in ideological matters mountaineers have a sense of humor.

In the Zone of Death it is not just one's breathing that is affected. The mind is not so fettered by the bonds of reason as it is lower down and seems to roam freely, sometimes on the very verge of sanity. But there is nothing terrifying or menacing about this mental condition; all it means is that the lonely summits seem to shed something of their remoteness. Extreme cold and the lack of oxygen—and more often than not total exhaustion—engender a sense of euphoria and complete indifference and conjure up visions of friends in need, "phantom comrades" so to speak. On his lone climb of Nanga Parbat, Buhl heard a voice warning him that he had dropped one of his mittens. Was it a sixth sense, the unconscious mind, or help from departed friends? And on Mount Everest Frank Smythe was suddenly quite certain that Shipton had turned back, leaving him alone. He felt sure that an unknown friend was close to him, and this gave him strength and confidence. Looking up, he could see strange beasts like dragons in the sky, and he realized that his overstrained nerves were playing him tricks. He rubbed his eyes, opened them again, and the dragons were still there. On Cho Oyu we had no "phantom comrades," perhaps because there were three of us. As well as enjoying a limitless view of other peaks and of Tibet far below, we sensed a sort of peaceful communion with everything that goes to make up this world of ours. Blizzards, extreme cold, and nightfall were no longer our enemies; they were just manifestations of the universe. The sky toward which we had so laboriously fought our way vouchsafed us a feeling of harmony that we had never known before.

A strip from a Buddhist prayer wheel

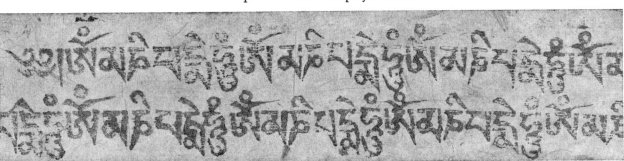

Glossary

ABDUR RAHMAN (1830–1901). Emir of Afghanistan 1880–1901.

ANGARALAND. Original North Asian continent, nucleus of present Siberia.

BAILEY, S. M. British geographer and naturalist.

BANYAN. The Indian fig tree, with its characteristic hanging roots. It is sacred because the Buddha reached enlightenment under its branches.

BECHTOLD, FRITZ. German mountaineer. Merkl's companion on Nanga Parbat in 1932 and 1934.

BHAGAVAD-GITA. "The sublime hymns": a book of the eighteen traditional Indian puranas (ancient chronicles); probably tenth century.

BODDHISATTVA. A being on the way to the status of Buddhahood. The multiplication of the original Buddha into innumerable Buddhas, past and future, was already apparent in ancient Buddhism.

CHANDRAGUPTA MAURYA (Greek SANDROCOTTUS); founder of the Maurya Empire. Reigned 321–296 B.C. as first ruler of all India.

CHANG. Beerlike drink made from barley by the Sherpas.

CHORTEN. A Lamaist shrine or monument.

CONTINENTAL DRIFT. According to Alfred Wegener's hypothesis, the movement of the lighter continental masses (sial) which float on the heavier, more viscous lower mass (sima). It is directed mainly westward, but also away from the North and South Poles.

DZONG. Fortified castle of a penlop or local potentate in Bhutan.

EMODON. Part of the Himalayas as described by Megasthenes, the ambassador of Seleucus I at the court of Sandrocottus, who compiled a four-volume work *India* about 300 B.C.

EROSION. The hollowing-out action of running water, which deepens and widens a channel. Retrogressive erosion: If a raising of earth masses interrupts the gradient, the rivers begin to cut through it, thus equalizing the gradient of their beds. The result is that the break in the gradient moves upstream.

FRANCO, JEAN. Well-known French Himalaya climber; leader of the Makalu expedition in 1955.

GONDWANALAND. Landmass in which Central and South Africa, Madagascar, and India were agglomerated in the Neopaleozoic period. Later the name was transferred to the great southern continent which stretched from eastern South America over Africa to India and Australia from the Devonian to the Jurassic period.

GUNSA. An additional settlement, lying lower than the main Sherpa village and used as a refuge in winter. Otherwise additional arable land.

GYALPO. Title of the Maharaja of Bhutan.

HAGEN, TONI. Swiss geologist; undoubtedly the greatest expert on Nepal.

HEDIN, SVEN (1865–1952). Swedish scholar, explorer, and writer.

IMAON. Part of the Himalayas as described by Megasthenes.

INDIAN MUTINY. The Indian rebellion against British rule; suppressed 1857.

IQBAL, MOHAMMED (1873–1938). Indian Moslem poet.

ISOTHERM. Geographical line of equal temperature.

JÖCHLER, SEPP. Tyrolese mountaineer; member of the Austrian Cho Oyu expedition of 1954.

KALIDASA. The greatest Indian poet; flourished fifth century A.D. Author of the lyric poem *Meghaduta* ("The Cloud Messenger").

KANCHENJUNGA. Third highest mountain in the world (28,216 feet); climbed by the English in 1955.

KUBLAI KHAN (1260–1294). Great Khan of the Mongols; from 1280 Emperor of China.

MANI-STONES. Stones on which the prayer *O mani padme hum* ("O Jewel in the Lotus Flower") is incised.

MERKL, WILLI. German mountaineer from Munich, famous for his attempts on Nanga Parbat and his tragic death there 1932.

MORAINE. Boulders and rubble shifted and deposited by glaciers.

MORSHEAD, H. T. Together with S. M. Bailey explored the gorges of the Tsangpo.

NIRVANA. The "dying out": in the philosophical sense the cessation of individual existence, in the religious context eternal bliss. In Buddhism and Jainism the final goal of the doctrine.

PADUTIN. Medicinal preparation against frostbite.

POTALA. Castle or fortified monastery of the Dalai Lama in Lhasa.

PURANAS. "Ancient chronicles"; the great Indian epics, consisting of eighteen books of a philosophical-religious nature. The main books probably tenth century.

RAJ. Hindustani: "rule"; hence maharaja, great ruler.

RANA. Powerful Nepalese dynasty which ruled the country for a hundred years.

RONICOL. Medicinal preparation against frostbite.

SADHU. Hindustani: holy man; generally a mendicant monk.

SAHIB. Hindustani: lord, master.

SHAMAN. Sorcerer in northeastern Asia or Siberia.

SHERPA. Tribe from the area around Mount Everest. See the chapter "The Great Mountain Guides."

SHIPTON, ERIC. British mountaineer; one of the pioneers of Himalaya exploration.

SIMLA CONFERENCE. Held at the Indian mountain health resort in 1904; produced treaty between China, Tibet, and Great Britain providing for the recognition and preservation of the Himalaya states.

SIRDAR. Leader of the native porters in a Himalaya expedition; in general an Indian honorific.

SUBCONTINENT. Part of a continent which by virtue of its great extent and marked separation from the remainder virtually constitutes a continent in itself, *e.g.*, India.

TETHYS. Central sea, covering South Asia, North Africa and South Europe, which can be traced from the Paleozoic to the late Tertiary period.

THEODOLITE. Instrument for the exact measurement of horizontal and vertical angles.

TIMUR LENG (TAMERLANE). Mongol conqueror; reigned 1370–1405.

TUNGAN REBELLION. Rebellion of the Moslem Tungan in Kansu and western East Turkestan 1861–73.

VARANGIANS. Norman tribe.

VEDA. Sanskrit: "knowledge." Oldest literature of India, consisting, strictly speaking, of four ancient collections of sayings and hymns (Rig-Veda, Sama-Veda, Yajur-Veda, and Atharva-Veda).

WEGENER, ALFRED (1880–1930). German geophysicist and meteorologist. Carried out four expeditions to Greenland, in the last of which he perished.

WEST-WIND ZONE. Temperate area between the polar wind system and the subtropical high-pressure zone in both hemispheres.

YOUNGHUSBAND, Sir FRANCIS E. (1863–1942). British officer and explorer. Crossed Asia and the Pamirs in 1886; 1903–04 led the British expedition to Lhasa; 1906–10 resident in Kashmir.